PRAISE FOR CRAIG SHERBORNE

'I read the first sentence and then pushed the day's work aside and sat down to read it all. I haven't come across such a lively and gripping memoir in a long time. Craig Sherborne has the knack of reproducing the soundtrack of childhood – that chorus of half-truths and received opinion that's always at our backs as we grow up.' —Hilary Mantel on *Hoi Polloi*

'This is writing of the first order, utterly controlled, utterly beautiful.' —*Sydney Morning Herald*

'Reading Craig Sherborne is an intense experience. His writing mixes pain and laughter, farce and tragedy. It skips from heart-breaking to ludicrous in a moment. It anatomises characters with almost indecent candour while showing a profound sensitivity to human distress. And in doing so, it demonstrates that Sherborne has an extraordinary eye for the damage, trivial and profound, that humans inflict on one another, that he is a great contemporary satirist and that he has a genius for the telling detail... *Muck* is an instant classic.' —*The Literary Review*

'Sherborne has created a narrator who is victim, supplicant, acolyte, a poignantly defiant rodomontade with a fiercely tender core, and it is a powerful, contradictory mix. *Muck* – pitch-perfect – bowls you over.' —*Book Review*

CRAIG SHERBORNE

MUCK

a memoir

W. W. NORTON & COMPANY

NEW YORK · LONDON

Copyright © 2007 by Craig Sherborne
First American edition 2010

For information about permission to reproduce
selections from this book, write to Permissions,
W. W. Norton & Company, Inc.
500 Fifth Avenue, New York, NY 10110

For information about special discounts for bulk purchases,
please contact W. W. Norton Special Sales at
specialsales@wwnorton.com or 800-233-4830

Manufacturing by Courier Westford
Production manager: Devon Zahn

Library of Congress Cataloging-in-Publication Data

Sherborne, Craig, 1952–
Muck : a memoir / Craig Sherborne. — 1st American ed.
p. cm.
ISBN 978-0-393-33790-7 (pbk.)
1. Sherborne, Craig, 1952– 2. Journalists—New South
Wales—Sydney—Biography. 3. Authors, Australian—
20th century—Biography. 4. Australia—Social life
and customs—20th century. I. Title.
PR9619.3.S4838Z46 2010
070.92—dc22

2009054280

W. W. Norton & Company, Inc.
500 Fifth Avenue, New York, N.Y. 10110
www.wwnorton.com

W. W. Norton & Company Ltd.
Castle House, 75/76 Wells Street, London W1T 3QT

2 3 4 5 6 7 8 9 0

muck

a memoir

IF WE'RE ALL born equal, why are some of us only cowboys?

I know why—an education.

Trackwork cowboys have no education. No wonder horse trainers mock them for such hard hands on a thoroughbred's mouth, a sack of potatoes the way they flap-flop in the saddle. Listen to the foul-mouthed fucks and cunts of their cowboy cursing, the mongrel-bastards of their horse-hating though it's dark dawn and no horse wants to walk faster so early.

They wear rodeo leg-chaps and Cuban heels. They put spurs out the backs of their feet like barbed wire. That's the difference between types like them and people like me. My trousers are cream jodhpurs when I ride. My skullcap is black velvet with a black ribbon trailing behind. My boots go knee-high. They're made of black leather, not gumboot rubber or fraying elastic sides. I've no spurs to stab with, I have a tongue to click-click up a rhythm.

They kneel over their mounts as if they can't do sitting. I have the straightest spine and join to the seat in my proper riding school way. I hold my hands down over the withers with reins threaded like so through finger and thumb. Like so over my pinkies to make a perfect U across the mane. My hips when I ride do little fuckings of the saddle and the horse rocks into me doing little fuckings back.

Cowboys. That's all they'll ever be, that's all they ever amount to my father says and I have no reason to doubt him, I can see it with my own eyes, even in Sydney at Royal Randwick—Royal before the Randwick like a king of names. But in New Zealand you expect it. Here they have no Randwick racecourse with its kingly name and Bart Cummings calling out the riding orders not some simpleton farmer. In New Zealand when you amount to nothing the nothing must amount to less.

Yet in Taonga, Churchill gives himself airs as if a real race-day jockey. As if a man of style, not another 4am cowboy. That polo-neck, I bet he bought it at an Op Shop. That anorak too, that polka-dot bandanna. His dented helmet droops on a slant, deliberately set at that angle to give him a look more debonair. How can he afford those Wee Willem cigars he's smoking as though he were an important man? One on the way out to the sand track for a canter. One every three horses like the smell of bad wood burning. He may have a scissor-thin moustache but that just makes him old-looking, not distinguished for all its greying. He's not distinguished and never will be in his life. He's a cowboy. He will always walk with a worried man's stoop. He is only here in Taonga because he did no good in England. If that wasn't the reason, why didn't he stay where he was born?

★

Taonga has only 3000 people but I have to admit those mountains are something—so higgledy with black-green forest and rockface when the cloud lifts from them by lunch. Forget the ugly mining truck tracks further to the south down Old Mana Road. Look at the mountains. They wall out the sky to the east. Somewhere deep inside them steamy artesian springs brew up and pour into the town's public spas.

Dairy farms everywhere. Pastures so greeny lush that cows can run two to the acre, and milk leaves a going-stale smell on the air. But Churchill is no farmer. He rides horses for a living in that hunched-over cowboy way. If you call his five dollars a mount a living even if he gets through ten horses a day, which he can't.

I know how much people earn. John, the manager of our liquor store in Rose Bay North, got $300 a week and that was Australian. On top of that he got a cash bonus when we sold it, and could always help himself to a good-will gesture of supplies. Five dollars is a pittance—this is 1977 not the Dark Ages. Churchill mustn't have had a good education even though he is English.

My father has the finest farm in all the district. Most farms
in Taonga are only 100 acres, but ours is 300. Ours milks
500 Jerseys and Friesians and needs a full-time staff of at
least two, which is unheard of. It has enough grass left over
from the cows for two broodmares, two yearlings and two
foals. It can make an income of over $80,000 if the man-
ager's modern, no peasant in his ways, no thinking cows
are pets not money. That's important because the farm is
our main source of earnings. My father gambles on horses
but gambling is just for play.

The lurks you get with farming, that's the beauty of it.
My father says "right on to the write offs" where his taxes
are concerned. Lurks can bring your taxes down to forty
cents in the dollar.

This place is why the liquor store was sold: what kind of
legacy is a liquor store for a son! A father wants to pass on
land. A father wants to create an estate and know that when
he dies his son will have that same land under his feet. It's a
form of never dying. A dynasty will be born, from father to
son, and son on to son and on it goes. A dynasty. Just like
the families at that school I go to in Sydney. Though with
us there's a difference. At my school the farm boys are called
Scrubbers because scrub is all there is west of the western
suburbs say the Sydney boys, The Citys. When Scrubbers
leave their grand boarding mansions to go home for holidays, they go home to drought and dust for all their owning

50,000 acres. What legacy is that to leave loved ones! What Scrubbers and their dustbowls earn our pretty sum!

Our 300 acres has rain on a string. Reach up and give a little tug on the air and the weekly watering will descend. Walk into a paddock and jump up and down. "Hear that?" my father whispers, putting his finger to his wide smile for me to shush and listen. "Hear it?"

Yes I hear it. Beneath our boots, beneath the very grass we stand on, the sound of water trickling like a brook.

When I tell Scrubbers about the water, about our 300 acres and 500 cows, the broodmares, yearlings, foals, they laugh at me to my face that I'm a liar—no 300 acres could feed 500 cows. That's a backyard size compared to their vast thousands. It's not something worth inheriting.

Because they all say it and none takes my side I worry that they're right—I'm only one against a dozen. I worry: have I dreamed it, Taonga? Do I spend my days confusing dreams with the real things? No, I *have* seen it, and listened and smelt it for myself. I say to the Scrubbers how superior to theirs our land is. But still they laugh.

I am beyond hating them. I don't want to think of them as alive. I wish them ill and ignore them as if they are dead already.

*

The dynasty has started with my father as the founding father and me his only son, the founding son. He looks forward to the day when he can watch his grandchildren out there in the clover-covered paddocks frolicking among the cowpats. Playing with a pony, getting stung by bees. The most wholesome activities in the world. And then when they get older, they'll chop a thistle or two, pull some rag-wort. Because it's important to get dirt under your nails. To sweat, to learn to work with your hands like a working man. Like the man he once was years ago setting out in life as a boy, and that going into business where you wear a jacket and tie has never made him lose sight of. All men should own a farm and be able to stand with an arm around their son and stare out across their domain, their manor, like the duke of all they see. All city men with their pasty faces, their limp as lettuce handshakes, they're not men at all. They're honorary women.

★

"It's all very well making a man of *him*, but you'll not be making one of me," my mother says. She's scrubbing the doorstep, and what a terrible thing for her to be doing at her age, fifty-three, as if she were a common housemaid doing chores, to keep this strip of timber as pale as pumice. But the step must be scrubbed because she can't be expected to put up with the muck that collects from paddocks, paths, what-have-you. The mud and cow dung ground into the wood grain like brown and green dye when staff knock to deliver the morning can of milk, or Churchill when he gets his fee. A stink to make your nose curl. A stink you cannot get out of the carpet when traipsed around on the soles of socks once we've bottle-opened-off our shoes on the door-step edge.

She cannot believe she was talked into this farm. What on earth possessed her to be talked into coming back to where she started—New Zealand. Even if it is only part-time, in school holidays, it is still New Zealand. We left New Zealand four years ago. We made all that effort run-ning a hotel among filthy-living horis, to make it a stepping-stone to a better way of life in Sydney. Somewhere where the "glamour" word had some meaning in the world with oysters at Doyles, with mink not mistaken for possum. With, with, with … she could go on and on. And yet here we are now back among peasants just so a man can pass on land to his son.

But it's not normal complaining from her. It's play-complaining. Pretend washer-women complaining while on hands and knees puffing hair strands from her eye with a phew of air. It's the play-complaining of knowing my father has no intention of making a man of her. He wants to make a lady of her. A proper kind. A lady farmer to his gentleman one. "A duchess to my duke," he bows like a regal fellow asking a dance of his ballroom bride. She places the rubber-gloved hand on his outstretched arm. They hold each other a little away from each other and sway this and that way, both singing a waltz of da-da-dums.

A duchess to his duke. She likes the sound of that. "Very fitting," she curtseys and resumes step-scrubbing. She phews that it can't happen fast enough, this duchess-duke business, or else he better buy her some curlers, cut her nails, take her teeth out permanently and go right ahead and call her the cleaner.

I've stopped calling her Heels in my head. Her Heels are bare and cracked now, chalky around the splits. Not teetering on their usual steeple but level to the ground, flat at the arches and rolled inward at the ankle like a deformity the high-heels kept in check. Her feet scuff along the carpet like static.

When did she ever bare her feet to me? Never. She was always Heels, like a cocktail glass for her feet. A glass that supported the whole of her, a glass she slightly spilled out of but was tapered into anyway.

She was Heels for that and her pantsuits—white, yellow, mauve and blue-striped. Pads upon her shoulders to broaden them. Legs not covered all the way past the knee but leaving a little of the tan shin showing. Collar turned up as if her neck was flaring. Clown makeup that wasn't meant to be clown yet her frowns and laughs stretched out that larger way.

To make so much of being pretty! She, the pretty-maker, has never cared that I, the son of her, thought it wrong. The way it made men watch her. She is my mother not a glass for others and their eyes. I'm almost sixteen, so I know

8

about eyes. Eyes aren't just for looking, for reaching a destination in a room without tripping or falling, banging into chairs. Eyes are for finding the body parts you want to watch on others. The sex-watching of breast, legs, buttocks, groin, lips, fingers. Just as the mouth is not just a mouth, a loudspeaker for weather-talk or football scores. It's for sex-charming and for pretending not to be by putting on a clean white smile as if merely happy to meet you. A smile that for all you know could be a silent punch, the leer of a killer.

Now she is just Feet to me. Feet I don't want to see exposed with their yellowings. Toenails I don't wish to glance down and notice so chipped, discoloured and splintery. Baby powder caked between toes. Shins that have itch-marks now, needing creams to stop them scabbing.

I blame the farm for bringing out this ugliness in her. Ugliness that must be in me as well, her flesh and blood, awaiting its time, its chance to show through. Will the farm do this to me next?

It's happening to The Duke as well. I can't think of him as Winks anymore. Winks for his way of saying "Just between you and me, son" with a blink of one eyelid, a man's equivalent of a kiss on the forehead.

He pulls a cap over his eartips to keep out the farm's freeze-burn of foggy morning air. He tucks his Jockey underwear elastics over his shirt-tails for the same reason. Never mind that the elastics show to the world. Who will notice in *this* world where everyone does much the same?

No suits, no hair-slick of shiny oil like a square, black other skin. His scalp is salt-and-pepper grey, there's a dry frizz at his temples. I blame the farm for him too. Hardly a duke in his trousers, once the lower part of a three-piece, now worn thin at the thighs and unthreading. His pockets ripped from hooking a hammer there because we have post and rail paddocks to build for the dynasty's horses: Flying Symbol, four wins and six placing, gave birth to Denovo (which means "start afresh" in a foreign language) who gave birth to Anew, star three-year-old colt in Bart Cummings's stable. Perhaps Anew, one day, when he finishes racing, will be foundation stallion in a post and rail corner of the farm which will be no ordinary farm. We will make it a showpiece.

★

We cannot quite afford to fence *all* the showpiece in post and rails, not yet. We are well-off certainly, but rich has its rungs. If we were the highest rung, then post and rails would be no object. But being the lower rung of rich means settling for fences we must make do with, fences made of wire that cuts your fingers when you staple it to the wood batons. The batons jab your skin because they're so shaggy with splinters.

We are, however, rich enough for a new house for the showpiece. The old one isn't falling down but at best it's a quaint house, a house Feet pulls a face in for being old-worldly: "Who has fireplaces anymore! We are civilised for heaven's sake. Every draught in New Zealand comes whistling down the chimneys. Who has frosted glass with flying ducks! Who has brass knobs and wood, so much dark wood the place is a mausoleum! As for floorboards—it's like we're too cheap to lay carpet."

The new house that will stand in its place will have all the mod cons. It may have a Tudor-style façade—white with brown criss-crosses—the architect's choice we've warmed to, but Tudor inside it is not. Houses come with more than one bathroom these days. Marble basins and vanities, or at least marble-patterned. Gold taps with your hots and colds in Italian.

Kitchens come with cook-top islands. We shall have a billiard room with red velvet wallpaper to go with the green felt of the table. A gallery with pink cane lounges where our descendants of the future can hang family pictures that will be there for all time. Not just stairs but a staircase. Central heating that you can't see since it is buried in the walls. Axminster, sable-blue and off-white. Six bedrooms, walk-in caverns for our clothes. A separate wing for the visitors we'll surely have. Relations will want to come and nose about. That's the thrill of having a showpiece—you can show it off.

The Duke unrolls the draftsman's drawings on the Formica table which will have to go for something better. He points out his favourite features: the entrance door will be a big swing affair. You'll drive up into an undercover area through a brown brick arch-tunnel arrangement. A landscape person will make red scoria gardens with plastic sheets to keep down weeds. There'll be lawns, but the smallest of the small of lawns to cut back mowing, lawns cool to stand on for Feet's tired strolling. All with a white post and rail surround high enough to stop inquisitive stock, but low enough not to obscure the new house from the road in that second it takes to glimpse it between gaps in the road hedge when you're driving past. If you've got a showpiece, why hide it?

"We must name the farm something," Feet says, sweeping her hand over the drawings, and sweeping again in a wider arc. "A house like this, and the whole farm around it, needs a name. We can't just go on calling it *The Farm*. *The Farm* is just for an ordinary old cow place, not a showpiece. Not the biggest in the district with a Tudor house for a homestead."

She sweeps in an arc another time. "If we go to the trouble to name a racehorse, then surely we can name all *this*."

That makes sense to The Duke. We could even have a plaque made for the entrance to the drive. Another one perhaps beside the front door. "Something that sounds—" He shrugs that he doesn't know what that something is.

"Something grand," sweeps Feet.

"That's it. *Grand*."

"Though it's not very grand having your Jockeys sticking up above your trousers," she says, eyebrows arched high and lips pursed to deliver a mild reprimand. "Trousers that really should be hung somewhere outside rather than be sat in inside, dirty and torn."

But The Duke's not listening. He squints down on a thought and mouths "grand" and "farm," then "Grand Farm," "Farm Grand," "Park Farm," "Park Farm Estate." Another squint. "Green Park" and "Green Farm."

Feet mouths what he mouths and tips her head to one side in contemplation, rejecting each name with a grimace like an unpleasant taste. Again she sweeps her arcs over the drawings. Slow arcs as if making a spell, eyes closed, with "Park" and "Estate" as the spell's magical chant. "Tudor" and "Tudor Estate."

"Tudor Estate. I like that," nods The Duke.

"Park Tudor. Tudor Park." She opens her eyes. "That's it. Tudor Park."

The Duke nods and mouths it over. "Tudor Park."

"Tudor Park."

"I like that. It's perfect. I think Tudor Park it is."

He bows and calls her "My lady."

CHURCHILL IS HERE to break in The Duke's two yearlings. His blue Morris Minor gurgles up the drive, over the zebra crossing of shadows the Monkey Puzzle tree lays down. He slaps a whip against his chaps. He straps his skullcap to his chin just loose enough so it tips in that debonair way of his.

He complains proudly that he's a very busy man and stoop-jogs to the stables. They are not really stables, though we call them that. Not the big garage kind with dozens of stalls either side. They're two horse boxes with a shared wall and new post and rail yard for a horse to look out on.

Yes, he's very busy because he has a little team of his own now—four young horses he's breaking in for locals, all under the one roof in an eight-stall stable he's renting just like a real trainer. "One or two of them show a good turn of foot in the paddock," he boasts, threading long reins like trotter's reins across the body of the first yearling, a black Denovo colt with an all white eye, a poached-egg eye, which means its temperament will be bad and must be fixed, beaten, broken. The Duke wants Churchill to work *around* the horse, not *through* him. If there's any beating to be done, it'll be The Duke who'll do it. That's his right—he owns the horse. Buy your own horse then it's you with the rights.

Churchill threads the reins from Poached Eye's bit through the saddle stirrups which are pulled down to full length to knock emptily against the creature's ribs and get it used to stirrups. He wants The Duke to know this: "If I can keep my team together, all under the one roof, instead of seeing them moved on to other trainers with a name, then I'll be set."

By *set* he means he too will get a name. He too will be someone they say has *reputation*. He flicks the reins against Poached Eye's flanks. He walks behind, steering like a man driving a plough.

Churchill makes the sucking, click-click speech that's Horse for "Walk."

"Come on, my darling," he quietly, tenderly commands. "That's my darling. There we are. There's a love. Good boy."

Poached Eye shudders and hops. His teeth crunch down on the bit as if eating a rock food. He doesn't stride smoothly but bucks and jabs with his hind hooves. The kinds of kicks The Duke calls "punching holes in the air." Churchill flicks the reins at this disobedience.

The Duke nods that he'll leave him to it. There are rails to be nailed to posts and then stained red-brown with a paintbrush. Feet's choice of colour because if it's good enough for the Queen in those magazine pictures of her riding, it's good enough for her.

I always step off in time with The Duke when he strides away, walking. I go in the same direction, at the same pace, a little to his side and a little behind. I expect this is what you do when you're next in line in a dynasty. Prince Charles does it with the Queen. He holds his hands behind his back which I have taken to doing though it's hard to keep my balance when travelling at speed. I hold them there until told to mind a hammer for a second, or help lift a rail when The Duke says "heave." I keep them there when he tells me to stand in front of the sun a while to block the glare for his better seeing of the work at hand.

But if I hang back at this moment I know what's to become of Churchill's darling-talk as soon as The Duke is out of earshot. I've heard him before. His darling-talk doesn't endear him to horses—Poached Eye kicks and head-butts the air regardless. Hate-talk at least enfears him: "Mongrel cunt. Mongrel fucking bastard. I'll teach you a lesson you'll never fucking forget."

When I tell The Duke that Churchill is talking about teaching lessons, he shakes his head, mumbles a curse and marches off to make sure hate-talk has not turned to whip-hate, to harming. But by the time he catches up, Churchill has always seen him coming. The darling-talk returns. The soothing, the fake-kindness commanding.

When the work is done, Churchill stands at the back door to collect his pay, skullcap under his arm like a military gentleman, something Feet says she approves of. He clicks his heels together when he talks to her which she also approves of. He calls her madam, which makes her give a polite bow of her head and which The Duke derides as "smarmy." As for that accent of his, his speaking in a toffy English way, it's got toffier since we've known him. That's why we dubbed him Churchill.

What Feet definitely does not approve of is letting him in the house. "We'd never get rid of him," she says with an eye roll. The one time he was allowed in he drank tea with his pinkie out, which is all very amusing and English to her. Then he asked if we had a nip of brandy. A nip of brandy in his tea to take the nip out of the air. Again, all very amusing and English. But she draws the line at his insulting us which, brandy or no brandy, he did last spring holidays. As if he being English automatically made *us* the lesser. As if a man who breaks horses was in fact too clever for the man who owns them, and for the woman married to the man who owns them. A woman more used to conversing with the better folk of Sydney, from judges to Cummingses, and whose son goes to a school we call The Mansions.

"The cheek," she grunts with a dismissive wave of her hand each time she thinks about the episode. *No one speaks* to her like that, she waves. No one says to her that he's mystified and appalled that we obviously have more money than brains. That if we can't see our way clear to trust him as trainer of the horses we breed, then we must be stupid.

"As if we'd give him horses of ours," Feet scoffs.

Churchill kept sipping his tea-brandy that day, wiping his moustache with the back of his index finger. "Don't you trust me?" he asked in an offended manner that made him bite his top lip.

The Duke replied that, yes, he was trusted, and got up from his seat to signal it was time for work not for more brandy and the prospect of heated talk.

"I always show up on time," Churchill said, and stayed seated. "I'm a drinker, yes. But so is everyone in this Godforsaken game. Give me your horses, damn it!" His small fist thumped on the table rattling the crockery's nerves.

Feet removed his cup though there was still a quantity to drink left at the bottom. Churchill reached out to retrieve it, but Feet was too quick.

The Duke spoke in the low, friendly but firm way he uses for staff, his business-is-business way. "You have to prove yourself first. Get a name."

"How can I do that if people like you don't give me your horses?"

The Duke said he'd think about it, which means No.

★

Churchill is what is called a Gunna. The Duke wants me to know this because I'll come across many such men in my life: Gunnas. Gunna be a great trainer. Gunna train a champion. Gunna do this, gunna be that. You find a Gunna in all walks of life. What do they have to show for their years on this earth? Nothing. Yet they think life owed them more for their efforts. They're what happens when you don't have an education. You end up a disappointed man, and die the death of a disappointed man, the death of too many racing men.

The Duke himself might be a racing man but he is an exception, he says. He himself may have little education but he has what is called *nous* and *savvy*. Old-fashioned get up and go in his bones.

This is not the sort of talk we have ever had—death-talk. I had no idea The Duke knew about death. He's the sort of man they call a doer, not a thinker. Not a contemplator on a topic for the poets. One designed for Keats, for Donne, not doers.

Like all men, I say excitedly, all men racing or not, they'll see their fortune in it, in death. The Duke is digging a post hole with a long-handled spade but stops his grunting and his stabbing at the soil and shakes his head at me, dismissive: "What do you know about death?"

I tell him I've read *Ode to a Nightingale* for school, and when John Keats says "Many a time I have been half in love with easeful death" and "Now more than ever it seems rich to die," I take it that he means he actually sees his fortune in death when most men strive for a fortune in life. I'm going to say as much for a class essay:

The wealth of no more need of money. The relief of no more hope or pride. No little emergencies of getting older, of continuing on alive.

The "pride" and "alive" are what are called assonance because I made the lines scan like a poem.

"What kind of stupid talk is that?" The Duke frowns. "Rich to die. No more hope or pride. That's … that's … defeatist talk is what that is. What kind of bullshit are they filling your head with?" he says, digging again, his voice juddering with the effort.

I tell him *they* didn't fill my head with it. I composed those words myself. They're my own. No hand-me-down scripture, no second-hand philosophy, but my words to have all my life.

He says he is not sending me to that flash bloody school for composing words of my own. For defeatist talk and poetry. "Where's defeatist talk and poetry going to get you in life? Where's it going to get you in business? Just as well we've got Tudor Park for you to fall back on. You'll need something to fall back on at this rate."

He stops digging and holds up the spade. "Here," he orders. "You can have too much of the wrong education. Let's sweat it out of you. Let's see you get your hands dirty with some good hard, pure work. None of your defeatist and poetry work. *This* type of work was what the word was invented for."

I take the spade and stomp its blade into the soil's soft black. Stomp repeatedly so the shiny edge is sent deep, deeper than The Duke has stomped it down, to prove I don't need the wrong education sweated out of me at all to do hard, pure work.

★

I'm going to say it to Churchill to his face if he's not careful: "You're a Gunna. Gunna go nowhere."

He is darling-talking Poached Eye, flicking the horse into a rocking, head-flinging walk. The breaking-in route passes behind the stable. Down the hill and alongside the pit gouged out by the front-end loader for burning rubbish to stop rats scavenging. When he reaches the pit he knows he is far enough off, and behind pit-smoke mist, to switch to hate-talk when Poached Eye bucks: "I'll show you a kicking in a minute you mongrel cunt. I'll kick your fucking guts out."

I'm going to catch him doing it. I'm going to tell him he better not move onto the next stage, the whip-hate stage, hate that sends a fist into horse ribs while the other fist grabs its ear and squeezes. I march over the straw-manure pile that spills down the pit's face. I stand a short distance behind Churchill, easily in earshot.

The Duke says a disappointed man, a man who has fallen short of his ambitions, takes the disappointment out on others—on wives, on children. Trackwork cowboys also have horses. I know this from watching Churchill. Cowboys may have no education but they know that to a horse a yelling, angry, disappointed man can be king of all its world. Such a king rules by forcing a steel bar in its mouth, he has a whip to punish its hide. He has straps that tighten around its belly, ropes to hitch up a fetlock behind the knee so the horse stands helpless on three legs instead of running away on four.

If still the creature won't bend to his rule, he fetches more rope, he fetches the baton with a loop of rope in it called the twitch. He grabs the horse's top lip and twists the rope-loop around it and screws and screws until the lip turns white and pain spreads deep into the horse, locks it in paralysed defeat. If there's still fight in it, another twitch will do the job, screwed onto its ear.

I'll make sure, when I address Churchill, that my voice is pitched low like a serious man's, my vowels round in the mouth, not a hint of nasal which would be unimpressive to someone English. My hands are behind my back as usual. I keep them there though I list off balance and slip on horse dung that bursts open with oats and chaff like a bread, a burnt bread, mouldy green and crusty.

"Don't talk to the horse that way," I say, I order. "Work around him, not through him."

If I tell Churchill to do something he has to do it, even though I am sixteen and he's a man of forty. One day Tudor

Park will be mine. In the line of the dynasty I'm second in charge. The only person who can tell me what to do is The Duke. He is the first in charge. I can't tell him what to do. Feet is a mother and not counted in rank and power.

If Churchill does not do what I say, then he would answer for it. He'd be *let go*. He is not king of me, it's the other way around.

He must be a deaf fool and hasn't heard me. "Work around him, not through him," I repeat.

Now he looks at me, I have his attention. He squints. His arms row the reins to bring Poached Eye to a halt. He laughs, a laugh snorted out of him, more a cough than a laugh, a belligerent cough that brings up sputum which he spits into the grass while looking at me. I make sure my chin is held high and my shoulders are square, my hands clenched behind my back, my chest pushed out. The stance of some-one in authority who better have his directives obeyed.

Churchill cough-laughs again and flicks Poached Eye into a prance. "I'm the fucking boss of you," he tells the horse, though surely it's really me he speaks to. "Come on you bastard, I'll show you who's boss."

Poached Eye rears and jumps sideways. Lashes out with his front hooves to strike Churchill though Churchill is too far away and continues flicking the reins and rowing: "I'm the fucking boss here you cunt." He flicks and rows again, flicks and rows as if trying to punish the animal with con-fused commands.

Churchill calls out to me, "You watching, boy?"

He then has the nerve to call out that I should look and learn how to show an animal who's the boss. After a fierce shake of the reins he kicks sods of caked mud at Poached Eye's behind, and roars, "Walk proper, you fucking dumb beast." He pulls down on the left rein to turn in a circle. Then the right rein, kicking sods and roaring at every falter. "Who's boss now?" he growls to the horse and scowls at me, kicking more sods for Poached Eye to trot up the hill away from me.

I must respond to this disobedience. How dare this disappointed man talk back to me. He, a disappointed man, has slighted me—my father's son. Me, heir to that horse, heir to this land. I refuse to be reduced to an inferior to a disappointed man. A man with no education. A failed Englishman. A Gunna.

*

I have to put him in his place. He doesn't realise what he is, a Gunna. Yet he needs to know how obvious it is for others to see it in him. He needs to know that when I order him to do something he better do it. No cough-laughs, no scowls, no spitting.

He has reached the stable. He flicks for Poached Eye to get through the gate, rows him to the right and flicks him through the horse-box door. His darling-talk has returned in case The Duke is somewhere about. But still he will manage one quick punch into Poached Eye's ribcage as his daily get-even. I've seen him do it before and I see the signs he has done it now—the horse is shuddering and fear-snorting when he should be snorting like a sigh, like relief that another day's work is done. Churchill's fist is relaxing back to being fingers. He unthreads the reins from the stirrups, leans down to unbuckle the saddle. He clucks and darling-talks for Poached Eye to stand quietly.

The horse-box floor is stripy with a few strokes of sun through the wall panels. Straw motes swarm and swirl. My shadow bends across the timbers, a skinny shadow, armless because of my hands being behind me. I begin to say, "You were told to work around him," but before I can complete the sentence Churchill turns his head to speak to my shadow, to speak over the top of me.

"So boy, what are you going to do when you grow up?"

I shuffle my feet. My hands have gone from my back to my pockets. I was not expecting questioning from him. Least of all that particular question. I don't have an answer for it. I'm under no obligation to answer questions from his type. He has no right even to speak to me about my private business. And to call me boy as if I'm junior to him. *Boy* when the truth is my height alone must be six inches bigger than his.

I do not have to answer him, but I do. I shrug, I shuffle and say "I don't know" without thinking. Without saying to myself first that here I am in the presence of a disappointed man and even *he* knows what he wants. He wants a reputation, a name. Am I in the early stages of being a disappointed man with my "I don't know"?

Doctor I should have said. *Barrister. Politician.* These are not lives that a disappointed man like Churchill could ever lead. They are occupations well above and ahead of him. They are what I should have said. Instead I've given him the opportunity to cough-laugh at me again. Worse, at the very moment he does cough-laugh he releases the saddle's surcingle with such a dangerous, deliberate jerk its elastic strap springs free like a slingshot towards me. It misses, but I feel its wind against my cheek.

Churchill undresses the horse of its rope and sack clothing, its leather and steel headdress. He saddles his arm with it all and grazes past my shoulder. A deliberate act of grazing, I'm sure of it. A challenge, the equivalent of poking or pushing. He has gone too far now. It's time to report this rudeness, this impudence to The Duke, these assaults on me.

That is exactly what they are—assaults. First the assault of insults—the cough-laughs, the scowls, the spitting which might have been a spit into grass but only an idiot would think it was anything other than a substitute he was using for my face.

Second, his deliberately letting the surcingle fling close to my face. I hate to think of the damage it could have done to my appearance, a permanent disfigurement if it had connected.

Third, the graze against my shoulder, outright physical contact. A violent threat to my authority, which is no less a threat therefore to The Duke's authority.

But would reporting these assaults lessen me in The Duke's eyes?

If I am the showpiece's heir, if I am to follow in The Duke's footsteps in the dynasty, isn't it for me and me alone to assert myself? Isn't it for me to enforce *our* rules and *our* way of doing things over a man who is no better than a common cowboy, someone so lowly he is hardly worthy of my hate?

THE CHESTNUT FILLY in the other horsebox is more advanced in the breaking than Poached Eye because, says Churchill, she is sensible.

"Hello Sensible," he greets her. "You're not going to give me trouble today, are you Sensible?"

He fits the headdress to her and she takes the bit into her mouth without struggle. She allows the saddle to be jiggled into the hollow of her back, its leather arm, the girth, strapped and buckled around her body's own breathing girth. He asks a question of her: "So tell me something, Sensible. What do you think *boy* here will end up being?"

Churchill nods and cough-laughs as if Sensible has whispered an answer.

"I see. Mmm. I think so. Yes, I think you may be right." He cough-laughs more theatrically, more mocking of me. "Yes, you're right indeed. He won't have to do anything. He can be a *nothing* because he's set up with a silver spoon in his mouth, and instead of work he can be a fucking gentleman farmer."

He leads Sensible from the horsebox to the yard to mount her for trotting figure eights. He cocks out his left leg for my hand to hoist him as riders do because they're small and need help in that way. For receiving help they should thank the lifter as a courtesy. But Churchill cocks and criticises me with "Come on, don't take all day" even before my hand cups the bony front of his ankle.

Now is when I must say it: "You're a Gunna. Gunna go nowhere."

But that won't be enough to punish him. There must be physical retaliation for his grazing me and the surcingle episode. I must pair saying "Gunna" this very second with his performing the little hop that begins his rising from ground level. A hop that signals I'm to take his child-like weight in my palm, stiffen my wrist and boost him higher.

"You're a Gunna. Gunna go nowhere." And as I say the "nowhere" I lift him, higher and faster than ever before. Toss him over Sensible's saddle like a piece of luggage onto a rack.

Churchill lets out a squeal-cry of shock and protest. He lands the other side of Sensible where hooves from figure-eighting have worn grass to an 8 of mud.

Sensible stutter-steps free of the commotion, snorting to gauge its warnings and messages on the air.

Churchill scrambles to his feet, making sure he's clear of Sensible's back legs, one of which is tucked ready for kicking as she pirouettes and bucks. He rushes towards me, waves his whip to let me know I'm in for a thrashing, so enraged no words form in him to make a voice. He is ten feet from me now. He shakes his whip madly, thrashes the air.

I hold up my fists. I walk backwards, faster, run backwards until I collide with the rail fence.

He stops. Shakes his whip like a bendy spear and cries out a vowel gutturally.

I am about to be beaten. I'm about to feel pain to my body and shame to my soul for being beaten by a disappointed man who thinks so little of me, fears me so little he'll take a whip to my skin. He couldn't care less that he beats The Duke's son and will pay dearly.

Churchill lunges, the whip flexing over his head to deliver blows.

I punch him. My right knuckles scrunch bone-flesh low down on his left cheek. He topples. His skullcap is pushed over his eyes by the fall. A blood trickle leaks from between his lips. He unfastens his skullcap, throws it to one side, blinks to clear his sight, sits to catch his breath.

There is a throb and ache inside my index knuckle from having made skewed contact. I've hit cheeks before—a dirty punch in rugby where with dirty punches you enfear. In bullrush at The Mansions and its toilets where you smoke and fight against your head being flushed. At first it's you the puncher who feels fear, fear that more harm was done to the fightmate than was intended. Churchill is so much older than those I've punched before. I cannot fear harming him, a grown man.

I'm not certain I have won the fight yet. But he does fear me, I think. He climbs to his feet and steps away from me. His hand swipes across the ground to retrieve his skullcap. He doesn't look at my eyes. He jog-walks out the gate, muttering to himself, though I hear it well enough, that I'm a mongrel cunt. Any self-respecting father would take me by the shirt collar and give me a thrashing I'd remember to my dying day. He turns and yells with his finger poking at me to emphasise every word that I'm mad, mad, mad. That's all I am. I'm nothing but mad. Then he leans off into a jog towards the house, calling for The Duke to come out if he's inside and hear what must be said about this mad son of his. "Mad, mad, mad," Churchill keeps chanting all the way to the back door where he flings open the fly-screen and knocks so hard he must be hurting his hand.

The Duke comes to the door, patting his hair flat from his day nap. "What's the racket?"

Churchill wants him to know this: that he refuses ever, ever, ever to set foot on this property again while I am allowed to follow him around like a spy, a watcher, a boy who thinks he's Master Muck. "I won't be talked out of it," Churchill says, though The Duke has made no attempt to talk. "I'm sorry but those are my terms." He takes a few hurried steps away as if to walk to his car and leave immediately. "There's nothing you can say to talk me around."

The Duke stands wedging the fly-screen ajar with his shoulder, bewildered by Churchill's fury. He looks up over Churchill's head to where I make my slow, slinking way to explain myself. He signals with a quick arch of his eyebrows that I'm to come to him at once.

★

I should have spoken to The Duke in the first place and there never would have been such trouble. I should have made it clear to him that Churchill's darling-talk soon turns to hate-talk and whip-waves, and when I tried to stop the behaviour in *his* name, as his deputy and heir to our dynasty, I was assaulted and spoken to like common dirt.

Yes, I should have let The Duke do the punching if punching was the thing to be done.

But I am not going to cower just because of a disappointed man, a cowboy and a Gunna. I have dealt with the matter myself, in my own way. The Duke will hardly think less of me for that. Quite the opposite. If I put my hands behind my back, breathe deeply through my nose to make my chest swell out, he'll see how worthy a deputy I've been.

He steps from the house to the concrete in his stock-inged feet. He wants to speak to me, just me. Churchill, if he wouldn't mind, should stand over there so that we two, father and son, can talk in private.

Churchill folds his arms and grunts that he's said his piece. He has no intention of repeating himself. He has said his piece, and he has made his position clear. He has laid down his terms and won't be talked out of them. No father can be blamed for having a mad son. "It's only out of respect for you, old sport, that I haven't left the property already. It's time to take that mad boy of yours in hand."

I tell The Duke that Churchill was one minute hate-talking and whip-waving at horseflesh and then for no reason simply turned on me. "Turned on me for no reason," I say, or venture rather than say, to test if what I'm telling him is being accepted as fact. I put plenty of puzzlement in my voice. Plenty of frowning on my face. I shrug, offer up my palms during the telling.

Churchill wants The Duke to know that the crux of the issue is respect. Respect for him, his skills and services as a horseman. But he has said his piece and awaits The Duke's response which he hopes will be firm action against this mad son he spawned.

The Duke asks me in a whisper, "Does he have a snitcher on you, do you think?"

"That must be it," I reply.

Churchill pulls his bottom lip down to show a bleeding wound. He mumbles, "Respect. Not a punch in the face." He spits blood-spittle to the ground. "Not deliberately throwing a hard-working man over a horse when all he wants to do is mount it and earn his living."

The Duke turns his back to Churchill, and whispers, "Did you do what he says you did?"

"No," I say, as if offended.

"No?"

"No," I assure him. "*He's* the mad one."

"The blood in his mouth came from where?"

"He fell off Sensible. He was probably drunk."

Churchill snaps his arms to his sides. "I heard that. That's a lie." He quick-steps up to The Duke. "Smell my breath. Not a whiff of alcohol, I can promise you."

The Duke turns his face away, grimacing.

Churchill speaks now in his toffiest style, a straight-backed stance, a proud pucker of the mouth: "Call your good lady out here, if you please. Let her smell my breath. Let her discover her son's mad, mad, mad."

The Duke says he will do no such thing. "Just calm down and drive away home for the day. Let the dust settle."

Churchill bows his head and spits onto the concrete. "So that's it. Blood's thicker than water. Believe *him* over me. Fair enough. If that's the way it is. Goodbye. To hell with the lot of you."

He swivels on his toes and stoops toward his car, muttering that I'm a mad, useless good-for-nothing, and he doesn't know why he bothers lending his services to people without an ounce of respect for his talents or a brain in their fucking heads.

The Duke takes a long, sighing breath and lets it out and says, quietly, slowly, "You *should* have hit him one."

"Should I?"

"Serve him right with all his to-do."

This could be a trap. Is he trying to trick me into confessing? He has just lost the man who breaks his horses. What a fuss in a small town to find a new one. I best say I kept my temper no matter how much Churchill provoked me.

Or would The Duke prefer to hear I held my own? If so, now's the time to say so. And to say it I will need an ashamed look to me for having lied. Innocence in the eyes, a bowed head and a soft pleading in my voice: "It all happened so fast. I hope I didn't hit him."

The Duke stares at me. His jaw bones grind in his face. Then he raises an eyebrow, amused.

I don't remember the details, I tell him, and rub my forehead in a sham-confused state.

Churchill's car wheezes without starting. Does it again. When the engine catches, it belches like a mock animal. It has to be let moan and fart to get going.

Feet has come from the house to see what the commotion is. She's been disturbed reddening her toenails with the mini brush that smells like sweet petrol. Her hair is bound in a checked scarf that is tied at the front because of a one-woman experiment she has undertaken. She wants to find out if there's a way to turn those old plain scarves that dairy farmer's wives turban themselves with to milk their cows into a fashion item of some un-peasant description. One she can transport to Sydney. A silk scarf would be easy—it's a given that it's snazzy. But what a challenge this check cotton is. And yet, with dangly pearl earrings it goes from peasant to pleasant.

Churchill's car-animal groans into a sudden, angry slide. The back wheels skid and kick up a spray of sods. Feet gasps, hand to her mouth, at what's happening to the driveway lawn of her future showpiece.

The Duke yells out, "Oi, steady on there!"

But Churchill makes the car skid and slide away leaving two gouged tracks which Feet calls out is "vandalism." She hurries to inspect the damage. Vandalism and grass murder, she calls it. "Nothing but utter loutish vandalism."

The Duke, however, is not concerned with lawn and wheel marks. He orders me to raise my fists, hold them mid-air, for his inspection. Not the fists so much, the knuckles and any signs of scarring and scratching. Signs of combat.

He identifies a red discolouration, a definite sign of trouble. A chip of skin he describes as "very admirable" and the sort you would expect to get when you connect, not flush but off centre on someone's chin. He smiles to the entire width of his top row of white dentures. "Goodness me. I didn't know you had it in you."

Feet wants me to get a rake and repair the vandalism before it has time to dry out and be permanent. But The Duke tells me to stay right where I am. "He's had enough for one day I think, love," he tells Feet. "He's learnt a few things today. About leadership. About taking no nonsense. He's got leadership qualities."

He smiles the whole white width again. More than smiles—his eyes, always so deep-set and dark, have a wet glow to them. A pooled lit quality that as he moves close to place his hands affectionately on my shoulders I see myself reflected in, in miniature as in two blurry mirrors.

I would never normally allow this physical move to be made on me, my shoulders embraced by him in a mother-like or love-like way that people do. A father should be a stone figure, twin of myself in looks and gesture. An older me whom I'm awed by but must secretly fight against and eventually overthrow.

But this mirror lock of our eyes is paralysing. The love-pride of a human for his next in line. The Duke can never feel this way about any other. I see it now—this power I have, that I, and only I, can be allowed by this man to have over him.

THERE IS AN example to set where the basics of hygiene and presentation are concerned. If the two head men of Tudor Park run around the place unshaven, what example does that set? Feet accepts that shaving is a horrible activity, scrape, scrape, scrape first thing in the morning. But if *she* can bear a blade across her legs for twice as long as we men take for faces, we should bear it too.

She accuses The Duke of not having shaved for two days. *Two days.* If he's attempting an impression of a rough diamond man of the land, he is doing a damn good job of it. The grey growth he has let age his face ten years stops her giving cuddles.

As for her son, he has such long strands of that granny-hair on his chin. He needs to become acquainted more intimately with the razor. She tugs the granny-hair and calls it "bum-fluff." I flinch away, but she has time enough for one twist and roll in her fingers.

Please, she beg-tells The Duke. Please get him into the bathroom and teach him to shave properly and more regularly. "I haven't seen his face smooth and clean in weeks.

You're both letting yourselves go."

She sighs, "My son will be shaving every day soon. Ah, milestones."

It galls me that there is no point to argue here. When she put it the way she has—that we two men of Tudor Park must set an example, that we shouldn't run around like rough diamonds, I can only agree.

Where's the little farce of fury we always perform? Where's my instinctive "No" or "Why?"

I must say it anyway: "No."

She responds with her usual narrowing of eyes, a suck of air through her clenched teeth, the bottom row of which overbites the top in yellow anger. She slumps into a chair. Her sharpened fingers make a galloping sound on the Formica.

For the little farce—the procedure and pleasure of it—I narrow my eyes back at her. I stick out my own defiant bottom teeth. I gallop my fingers, a more padded gallop than hers given her advantage of long filed nails.

Her twitching chin and tearless sob will be on display next. She will say, "What have I done to deserve this from my own son?" And, "After all I've done for him!"

Then The Duke will raise his voice to me, "You show your mother some respect."

He will put his hand on her knee and let her lean in under his arm. At that point the little farce ends. I do as he asks, because *he* asks it, not her. The chain of command has been restored.

The ceiling light hangs from a frayed, brown plait of rope. The only light for seeing in this toilet, bathroom, mirror place. Dim for shaving, but The Duke says he knows tricks. Tricks a father hands on to his son that makes the dark, when shaving, easy.

He steers me, hand on shoulder, to the pink sink where cracks in its bowl are so fine and grainy they could be hairs shed from washing. I'm to bend at the hip, bend forward like so, till close enough to the mirror to see cheek pores.

Off with my shirt, off with my singlet so when we wet the soap it only splatters onto skin.

On the sink ledge his shaving brush with worn wooden stem. Its dried hairs candle-flame shaped with the foam of his last using it. Beside it his razor—a steel cross-bar whose miniature roof opens for blades, the ones he calls the Safetys.

He opens the cross-bar to show how a blade is more like paper than blade, being so thin and therefore so sharp. It lies flat in its slot with the merest edge protruding for cutting.

He runs water over his finger until the cold stream steams that it's hot. He waters the candle-flame. It drips open into a greasy brush again, a paintbrush to smear the white lather.

He taps me on the shoulder to lean back into his front. I do. Our breathing presses on each other. My stone-figure twin has paralysed me once more. He reaches across my right shoulder for me to take the candle-brush in my fingers and let his own fingers guide the way to make the circular rhythm as if mixing a spittle-froth on my jawline, throat, jaw again, chin, jaw.

Bubbles burst and tingle on my skin.

"Bite your lips back into your mouth," he instructs, demonstrating the liplessness himself and watching me copy in the mirror.

I'm to paint over the no-mouth three times; five times across my Adam's apple so as not to take the top of it off with the blade, only whisker slime.

Now grip the Safety's handle, pinched between fingers limply, not as tight as I do. Again his hand guides mine. He repeats the word "limply". Most things you never grip in a way you'd call limply—a handshake for instance—but this is one time the word is most suitably applied. He says it quietly as a whisper, and with sweet-tea breath. "The blade must glide your stubble away, not dig in and draw blood. Glide, not stiffly, not deeply."

I can hear the scratching carry faintly in my head. The almost-pain of cutting. The Duke reminds me that if I go too fast I'll be wounded. If I go too slow the blade will tug instead of shave.

He tells me to extend my middle finger and trace over the shaving path to feel for misses. You don't need strong bulb light to check for misses. You just need a follow-up with your fingers. "Feel it?" he breathes. "Need another swipe for good measure?"

"No," I breathe back. "We got it all."

I'm to puff out my cheeks now, one cheek at a time. This is to get access to cheek whiskers which need to be coaxed from hiding in cheek softness. He peers into the mirror, his cheeks puffed out in leadership of mine.

Now stick out the chin and screw the mouth up to push the chin forward further. The top lip should be stretched over top teeth. Now the feel-test. Then a final trim near the ears, squaring the sideburns with a firmer flicking downwards motion.

"Rinse your face off," he says.

Foam smears the bottom lip of my ears. The Safety has left a peel of lather behind the lobes. My sideburn fringes wear a straight milk moustache. I'm to rinse it all off with warm water, one rinse. Then a rinse with cold to close the whisker holes.

Pat the whole works dry with the towel. "How does that feel?"

"Tight," I reply. My face-skin is itchy.

I'm to hold out my palm for a squirt of Q-Tol, its menthol, cough-lolly smell.

"There you go," The Duke declares. "Finished. Done. You're a new man."

Feet insists we come out into the kitchen sunlight so she can look at her new man herself. "Where's my handsome man?" she fusses, leading the way to the sun. "Stand there so I can see."

Her hands are clasped in front of her. She blinks and smiles. She touches my face to feel for smoothness. "Look at you. You've gone from scraggly to feeling all womany. You're exactly like me when I was younger. It's like I've been given the gift of a daughter." She sighs and shakes her head. "You've got my face. Look at you. Those cheekbones, they're not your father's features. I'll give him your nose. He can have that, It's a bit too biggish. He can also have your ears. But those cheekbones, *I'll* have those. And those eyes, and that brow. And as for your mouth—they're my lips to perfection, that lovely zig-zag they do. A mother knows her child is herself, and here's the proof: your face in mine, and me in you."

IF I LIVED in better times, there'd be a war to go to.

Instead there are the Churchills of this world to put up with. And workers of such low rank they work in stink. They wear gumboots because of cow muck where they walk. Green porridges of it, watery and arcing out of cow backsides as if from a hose.

History does not happen here.

In grander times I wasn't needed. The Napoleonic Wars did fine without me. The birth of England. Men had the plain names we still have now but in 1066 a William was a conqueror. A Norman was a state.

There once was a Troy, a Troy that was a poem for the great Greeks, not a flash name for boys because the Johns and Marks and Josephs became too usual. A Helen was a sacred face. History does not happen to me. I wasn't needed to be alive in Mycenaean places.

So why now, why put me here in this time and place where the Normans and Williams merely milk cows and my duke thinks it's wise if I do too. We have a manager called a sharemilker who is meant to hire and fire staff, but this is *our* land not some sharemilker's. We trust family but no one else: "I want you to be my eyes and ears among the workers," winks The Duke. "You can learn what's good for business. You can tip me off to any laziness or graft."

I am considered no better than a milker of cows. What an insult to me! Whatever power or fate or science decides who drops to earth, in what place, what era, it considered me fit only for this—for milkings.

The power-fate-science decided a long-bow was too difficult for me. This boy couldn't lower a gun-sight. No shield or mallet for him. No cannon to scream, "Fire!" Not even defeat, not even the *Last Post* and Gallipoli.

My armour is a Swanndri—a black and red check bush coat to keep out rain and wind, the piss-splashes on concrete from a simpleton cow.

Is this why we study history, to envy the dead as if they were our betters?

Well Betters, let me dig you up in your millions, there in your unmarked graves in the earth's layers. Let me stick you back together and be treated to these three square meals a day I have. Have my soft bed, my electric blanket, my idle evenings with a book, and *you* go into that milking shed. *You* touch those simpleton cows.

There they stand against the steel, jagged rails called the herringbone, concertinaed side by side in the spaces the jagging makes. Forty-eight at a time, half to the left, half to the right. *You* touch their bony backs. You watch their arm-long tongues lick snot from their nostrils.

They are patients having their bodies drained like an illness. Those hairy, scabby udders between their legs. Men's genitals of sorts—a scrotum and four fat penises. They have penis tails where their real tails were lopped. These lift up exposing pink-inside vaginas, hairless except for a wispy spout at the end. A deformed man and woman in one, that's a cow.

Friesians are black and white at once. Two pigeon-toes for each foot; heads de-horned to horn stumps. They are taller than Jerseys, whom the staff call better natured with their eyelashes much longer to be "the more feminine of the girls." Weaker too for yanking into place in the jaggings. You grab a knob of their spine and just pull. They obey. If they don't, their penis-tails are easier to lift erect so that their backs sink down and they surrender as if in a wrestling hold, powerless, anus contorting like a puckered-shut mouth.

Friesian penis-tails are more difficult to lift. They lock against their vaginas and it takes two hands to lever off.

"They all kick," says Norman with a crackly cough-up of words and smoke. "Your quiet Jersey. Your mad Friesian. They all kick."

He keeps his tobacco in a round tin like a culture. It could be cuttings of his ginger beard and chest hairs. He smokes it to the dark-brown last of the rolling paper which sticks to his bottom lip like the top off a sore. What a low rank he must be. So old—at least sixty if a day, and still only milking cows for his wage.

He wears short pants for this warmer afternoon weather. Just below his knees the tops of his gumboots have worn hair away to a permanent ring. A watermark from standing so long in the world. This wet world in a pit where we stand with cow feet at eye level.

He doesn't smile or laugh. He only talks because he has to, because he's been told to instruct me about cows kicking your arms away when you reach in with milking cups. About using the spray-guns hanging from the rafters, a quick squirt of water at the udders and a massage-wipe to tease the milk down. When you transfer the cups from one cow to the next you must dip them in a bucket of green iodophor disinfectant. This way mastitis, if there's any, isn't spread among the herd.

You test for mastitis with your forefinger and thumb. Norman pulls on a teat for a squirt of milk to come. He's not embarrassed doing this, to masturbate this teat-penis. He caresses it, then masturbates all four on the cow. He does this in front of me, so casually, this most intimate of things. If the milk turns blue on contact with concrete, the cow is pure and uninfected. A cloud or clot, a greyness of impurity, means a red cross must be sprayed on the udder, the mark for medicine.

Norman's son is a William. Not even that—a Bill. He wears a flannel hat, the kind his father wears, pale-blue and frayed from many washings. His yellow hair hangs from it to his shoulders, half a dozen main shreds hardly worth keeping. He works at the other end of the pit attaching cups to penis-teats as if holding apart a cat's-cradle of rubber. He flicks his wrist and the cups suck their way on. A white gush pulses inside the cup's spyglass window.

Surely his father is a disappointed man. His son, a grown man himself, follows in his footsteps, but what legacy is this? It's not the same as mine. Theirs is a man–cow intimacy, an unembarrassed touching between legs.

Mine has no intimacy at all. I am a businessman. An educated man in the making. I have been given a job by The Duke, an eyes and ears responsibility. I should be friendly to this man and son couple, this Norman and his Bill. But that's not the same as being one of them. They themselves will realise I'm not of them, and never will be. Just as the cows will sense I am not the usual rough toucher between legs, but someone respectful enough to turn his head away and not watch where my hands go. Even whispering an apology when my fingers make contact with the dangle of skin.

"I have a duty to learn the business," I think, eyes squeezed shut as if the cow will absorb the gist of my thinking, my head being so close to its heart.

Any reasonable cow would forgive me this physical contact and apologise back for my being placed in this demeaning position. She would chew the cud lump at the side of her mouth and shift her hind leg for my better access without me needing to tap it and ask.

★

With the cat's-cradling of cups it is impossible for me to keep my hands behind my back in my Duke's-son stance. But at least that exposes my fingers to these two rough touchers, fingers so obviously different from theirs, not scarred and red and wrinkly as the teats they handle. My nails have no dirty ends beneath them. I clip dirty ends off, scrape the quick clean in the bath.

Norman and Bill may have knowledge, but it's cow knowledge, hardly knowledge in the real sense, the book and history sense. Let them have their knowledge and consider they've got that over me if that's what they are thinking in their frayed flannel heads. I couldn't care less. It's not Napoleonic knowledge. It's not the Magna Carta, it's not *Paradise Lost*, it's cows. It's manual work and habit and the drudgery of years. Of making milk come from the mud and grass of paddocks that just as easily ends as dung. It's knowledge of no importance except that mastitis causes "gradings" which means this day's harvest of milk is poisoned.

Just to be sure they're aware I have a superior knowledge level, I pat my rubber milker's apron which hangs from my throat to my ankles. I say, "It's hardly chain-mail is it?" But I must curb my tongue. "The Normans would never have attacked Saxony in *this*." That's enough. I mustn't say another word. "I suppose they had their milkers in Saxony." I don't want to humiliate these rough touchers. They might walk off Tudor Park. I'd be blamed for there being no touchers. "I suppose they had them at the Battle of Hastings, bringing up the rear without swords."

Norman licks his paper sore to the other side of his lip. He keeps silent except to say "Settle" to a Friesian who has been sucked dry and needs her cups removed. He kinks a rubber air-hose across his fingers to cut off the suction, pulls the cups from the udder and dunks them in iodophor. Two foamy thrusts. The cups are ready for cat's-cradling to another cow, for milk to spin through the cups' spyglass in time with the machine's suck-pulsing.

If I was asked to give a report to The Duke on Norman and son, I'd say they are a simple people. They are at home with cows. They don't want trouble. They won't talk back.

THERE IS OBVIOUSLY no such thing as rural hospitality, says Feet. We have owned Tudor Park for how long now? Eighteen months? And not so much as a scone, a cake, a sponge has been offered as a welcome. Not so much as a neighbourly knock on the door. You'd at least think someone would invite us for a drink. Or simply a cup of tea if they had any decency. It wouldn't kill them to be civil. "I know they're out there," she shudders and gives herself a warming hug. "I can feel their eyes on me."

She can feel the eyes when she stands at the front window trying to get a bit of heat from the sun. Out there, among all that green—green hedgerows, green trees, so many green paddock rectangles. She imagines neighbours' eyes staring through their curtains. Across the road the old couple with the elbows out of their jumpers. Their son and his wife who live in a house the size of a garage. How can they possibly inhabit a house so small! Not fit for a midget to live in. The wife—what a face-ache, Feet shudders. Barely waves if she passes you on the road.

Even the mountains have a staring look about them. But a mountain's just a mountain and can't help it. Not like the staring treatment you get at the local store. Feet has never seen mothers so young. They are girls not woman, yet they wheel babies of their own *and* have one on the hoof *and* one ready to drop. Breasts so big you could put cups on them like cows. Not a skerrick of make-up. Lank hair you think they'd do something with, perm.

"Mind you, the man behind the counter always smiles when I come in. You know why? I'll tell you. I pay cash, and cash is a man's best friend."

The district, so The Duke has heard, has a fair lot of Brethren. "Close knit," he calls them. Feet calls them "cliquey."

"Where are the binoculars?" she wants to know. The Duke's racing binoculars that see to the earth's end. His aftershave soaked into the rubbers from so much racing. They're hanging in his wardrobe. They'll be perfect for a little staring of her own.

"You can't go doing that," The Duke reprimands and laughs at the same time which only eggs her on. "No one's staring at us."

He walks away shaking his head and laughing that she wouldn't like the binocular treatment herself.

She says she doubts any of these types would own binoculars in the first place or even know what binoculars were.

She draws the front window drapes closed, leaving open just enough of their rose pattern to point the lenses through the gap and peer across the green outside world to search for eyes.

"Let's see. Face-ache and family over the road? No. Can't see any evidence there," she mutters, squinting for better focus. "What about the mailbox people?"

The mailbox people are the others living along the road. Those Feet has never met in person but knows by their mailbox names. "Dutch and Yugoslav or one of those breeds—Van der this and Such and Such avich that."

She lowers her arms for a short rest, hooking the binoculars over her wrist like a handbag. "Would you help?" she asks, a grinning invitation to join in on her fun.

"Your teenage eyes could see right into their lounge rooms."

And they can. I can see Face-ache's lounge blurred in the binoculars' insides. A dark sofa, but no eyes.

Then there is Norman and son's house which is our house really, one of three we own for staff. In the binoculars' telescope its side window is open. A shadow-head passes it, a woman—Norman's wife?—minding her own business, bending, perhaps cleaning or at prayer.

"What do you see?" Feet asks, anxiously.

"Nothing."

She places her fingers across my fingers to take back the binoculars.

I resist and scan the mountain ranges where clouds are always foaming like great waves in the act of breaking.

Clouds blank-white in these lenses. Rock grey and wrinkled with wet shine. Tree-tops so thick together they could
be moss or slime.

Turned the other way around the binoculars are a micro-
scope for squinting far off into the world to view its zero
of horizon.

Feet tugs at my hand. "Stop playing with the damn
things. You should be helping me. Look at the mailbox
houses. Or at Face-ache's again. Can you see anything?"

"Yes," I say, pretending something has caught my eye
at Face-ache's.

"What is it? Let me look."

She grabs the binoculars from me and leans through the
gap to see for herself. "I can't see a thing. What did you
see? Was she staring from her lounge at us?"

"Yes," I lie, clenching the muscles in my stomach to lock
down laughter.

"I knew it. I can feel their eyes."

"Do you think they try and stare through our windows
while we're undressing?" I clench.

Feet lowers the binoculars. "God, I never thought of
that. Undressing. How disgusting."

She hurries to her and The Duke's bedroom and jerks
the rosy drapes shut to make safe dark. If I'm to tell her
I've seen no eyes, no staring from any lounge, it should
be now. Before she gets "worked up" as The Duke calls
it. Before the two steps one way, two steps the other she

takes as if worried there is some place she must suddenly rush to but where it is, she doesn't know. Dig all she can with her fingernails into her scalp, she doesn't know. Have her headscarf fall free as she digs and scratches, still she doesn't know. Her hair-bun sprayed solid as a bird's nest can spill out its bronze pins but she just doesn't know. And not knowing makes her mutter with spit on her chin. Makes her cry out and swear the coarse words she is usually appalled to hear from others—bastard, shit, prick, gutful, arseholes.

There is a dangerous pleasure I have watching her. She, my mother, has a second self behind the pinned, sprayed one I know. It sees what I can't see—the eyes of others, for instance. Feels them chill her skin. It tells her to take a ghost train ride inside herself—I've come to think of it that way; her spine the narrow, plummeting tracks.

I want to join in and glimpse for myself what devils jump out of the darkness. There is no need to be scared: Feet always returns safe and happier than before, as when she steps from the shower whistling after an invigorating wash. She says she's sorry for anything she said but it's normal for people to let slip bad things and she vows never to do it again.

If I held her hand, could I ride down too? When I've tried in the past she pulls her hand away.

Quick now, it's time to confess I didn't see anyone: "It was just a speck on the lens."

But it's too late. She yells for me to shut up because she can see what I'm up to: I'm lying to her that I saw no one when I really did. Lying to make her look a dill of a woman who feels people staring. That's what I'm up to. She knows it. She can tell. "Get away from me you lying shit." She waves her arms wildly and stomps.

The second self is taking her away.

The Duke has arrived to catch her hand, to hold her back, to keep her here. He calls her "love" and "dear," but her hands are not for his hands now. They're for jabbing in her hair.

"I won't be snubbed and stared at by bastard pricks of peasants," she sobs tearlessly. "I'll do it myself, I'll make my own welcome. You bastard shits, I'll welcome myself. I'll do it myself!" she screams at the window as if beyond it to people.

I HAVE A twitch self. Is that the same as a second self?

The minute Churchill returns, it comes into me. Barely forty-eight hours and here he is because he needs the money, can't do without the work.

I don't wish to stoop to his level but it's obvious he is in my twitch. Not a twitch screwed on to his top lip or his ear. There is no rope-loop to subdue his body. It's invisible, this kind of twitch, yet it has twitched his tongue into silence. Not like him to thread the driving reins through nervous Poached Eye's stirrups and say nothing. There is no darling-talk from him like man-to-horse pretend love. No hate-talk once The Duke's earshot has been cleared.

I am as good as having The Duke around when I stand near Churchill now. I am The Duke in lieu. I hardly need to keep my hands behind my back to demonstrate it. I don't need to speak though I'm tempted to say "Work around him, not through him" as a test to observe if he fights against it.

I could be friendly, praise his skill as a horseman. Release the twitch's grip a fraction to see if he expresses gratitude, says thank you with a courteous smile, or merely shrugs and goes about his business.

But it's enough to have Poached Eye buck and mouth angrily at the bridle. He senses Churchill is not his king anymore. He is not the same king he was, this silent twitched one. He is weak and only commands with small rein flicks.

Given his weakness I am willing to forgive Churchill his insults and mockery, the deliberate surcingle grazing. I would take the twitch off him, but how do you remove what isn't really there?

What is there is the natural order of things, and to remove that can't be done. Churchill understands my superior place in it now.

★

It's the same in the milking shed, with Norman and Bill.

I want them to feel they can speak to me as they would speak to someone in their vicinity. But nothing too private that might disturb the natural order.

My school as a subject or the books I've read are acceptable. The rugby position I prefer to play—blindside flanker. But no family prying. I would certainly never mention Feet's second self. No "Do you wish you had some brothers and sisters? It must be lonely when you're just the one" from them. The usual nosing of elders.

"No," I would answer as always to that question. "I've never known different." I keep to myself the truer answer:

I would detest a brother or sister. They might steal my rank and rights.

It's unlikely there would be tales of sex-fucking from them—a father and son in each other's company. I'm willing to let on I have had sex chances, but stop short of admitting my virginity.

There is also the natural order of the smile.

I mustn't smile too much in their presence. Especially if they attempt vulgar humour or foul-languaged jibes. That would simply reward their presumption that I wouldn't be offended.

Feet has a particular way of pointing out the flaws in others. She does it to their face. Does it for their own good. Does it with a half smile while not looking them directly in their eyes because that would be too hostile. She looks somewhere past them, a little over their head, and says, "Where I come from we don't do that sort of thing." She says, "Where I come from we have saucers for our tea-cups and would never use a mug." "Where I come from we have the TV turned off while we're eating."

The next time Norman lifts up a penis-tail I intend to say, "Where I come from we use our heads not our brawn. We work *around* them, not through them."

I admit that Norman is probably right when he says it's easier to milk cows if you look at what you're doing instead of looking away in the hope your fingers can finger the cups into place. If you don't look at what you do, you fiddle and fiddle and the cups miss their mark. But does he have to remind me of this over and over? I grit my teeth against reminding him that where I come from we don't repeat ourselves, we don't make the same obvious point more than necessary. Especially if we are only staff.

Instead I say, "Where I come from we don't bother with *these*," meaning cow udders. "That's someone else's job."

A Friesian keeps fending my hands away. It paws my forearm, scratching me with the blunt pincers of its pigeon toes. Still, I have done it. I have attached all four cups without having to look down and witness myself in the act of doing so.

But Norman coughs into speech that I crossed them up, the cups. The far-rear one is milking the near-rear. The near-rear one is hanging loose milking only air. He leans over to correct the crosses but I smile past him that this is my cross, thank you, and therefore mine to uncross. He crackles that I would be better off standing straighter to the side of the beast, not in line with its back leg and too near its backend: "Unless you want to be kicked, or worse, get a shit shower for your trouble."

He shares laugh-banter with his son about me. He says we'll be here all day with my cross-ups and not-lookings. He says I should learn to use my wrist when I work. I should hook it into the crook of the cow's hind leg and force it from the ground so the cow knows I'm the stronger. "Put muscle into it," he crackles. Then without my requesting it he steps in front of me, shoulders me out of the way and cat's-cradles the cups himself. He then walks along the pit to cat's-cradle others.

I follow him determined to prove that *my* method of cat's-cradling, the not-looking method which is the only way I can tolerate the whole activity, is as good as his. I choose a Jersey, those better-natured eye-lashes. Jerseys' penis-teats are boy-small, half hidden in a thatch of fawn hair. I apologise to the cow for what I am about to do, and then begin the cat's-cradle with my eyes winced closed.

But the apology means nothing to her. And despite guiding the suction to her milk-pizzle with the gentlest fingertip stroking, the Jersey flinches and kicks and catches the claw of the cups between her toes. She stamps the cups to the concrete and I instantly give her my own kind of kick, a reflex flick with the back of my closed hand on her thigh. A reflex but with enough calculation to make sure I kept the flick contained to just a flick so it will go unnoticed by Norman and son.

Now it is me I apologise to. For losing my composure. This cow has no thought for my feelings, no thought for the sympathy and respect I showed her with my not looking. And if this boy-teated creature kicks me again there's no telling what I'll do. I might give her another flick, a firmer one. I might let myself make it a wild, hard fist-hit that Norman and son can see for themselves for all I care. Let them see that I can stoop to their level if I need to, if provoked, if not treated the way you should treat someone in my position at Tudor Park. I may have thin white fingers but my hand is strong enough to wrench any bony stump of a tail and bow a cow's back down.

"You wouldn't need to do that if you looked at what you were doing," says Norman with a wheeze and a victorious tone, a smug monotone.

"Do what?" I reply, staring at him with all the puzzlement I can pretend.

"The cow leg." He slaps his hand across the air to demonstrate my secret flick.

I smile past him that he is mistaken. "Where I come from you work around them, not through them."

"And where exactly is it you come from?" Norman is now speaking an octave lower, as if speaking down to me.

"I come from Sydney."

"Oh do we," he crackles to his William, his Bill who mumbles "Sydney" back as if there is something wrong with coming from Sydney.

Norman points to my forearm where blood trickles from a scratch I had not felt the pain of. "Where I come from you dip that sort of thing in iodophor," he says.

If I was to report on Norman and son I would say they're a snobbish people. Not as docile as I first thought.

Norman particularly has a tendency to speak his mind. Someone like him, a disappointed man with no education to speak of, milking cows at his age, and his son doing the same, should be grateful for a job at Tudor Park.

If Norman has trouble cat's-cradling a cow, his Bill will step in and, risking a hoof-kick, lift a penis-tail to help. His father does the same for him. Did they step in to lift for me? Not once. And now I have an embarrassing wound.

I was right about cows—deformed men and women, that's what they are. Mean with men and women hearts.

A BELL RINGS, out the side of my sleep. A dull clanking ring. Not a real ringing now that I wake, but the grating chafe of pots and pans, plates and cutlery.

There is the smell of burning—of cooking, and cooking gone wrong.

With waking, the sting begins in my forearm. I have no intention of treating the wound with anything more than spit from my mouth. *This* will be my first farm scar. How could I think it embarrassing, this O shape on me. It might only be as deep as a wrinkle but I'm confident it will leave a purple crust that festers nicely, and underneath the crust a paler purple signature of hard work to show forever.

If I worry that it is healing over without leaving a mark, I will pick and scratch until the skin re-opens and infection worsens the weeping.

Then from the Normans and sons of this world to the skinny Citys at The Mansions, the wound will be noticed and the noticer will think: here's a man who not only can work with his head, here's a man who can work with his hands. The scar says *Strong* and *Vigour* to the world. It says

Brave and *Dangerous*. It has a story with it of cow hooves and kicks.

I must get more of these scars on my hands, perhaps my face. One across my cheek would say *Daring*. I must also let dirt pack under my nails.

Feet is splashed with white powder—her hands, her forehead. No, she has not had an accident with her make-up, she assures me. "This is flour," she says.

She pats her hands onto her apron. The first time I've seen her wear such a thing. A blue and red check one with frilly edges. The apron is called Nanna's. So are the piles of letters she is reading. "These are your Nanna's recipes," she says in a soft, reverent voice. "Haven't looked at these for years."

She begins to sing, "Just a closer walk with thee." She sings those six words only and hums the rest of the tune.

The recipes are written in a curly feminine hand. Some are typed in blue print with oversized full-stops, club-foot commas.

"Cream of Tartar, 2 level teaspoons," Feet reads.

"It's after midnight," I complain.

"I'm aware of that. You should learn to sleep like your father. Minus the snoring. One teaspoon of sugar."

"What are you doing?"

"I'm working on my welcome."

Brown, misshapen rocks of flour with burnt bases fill the rubbish bin.

"Flour sifted. Done that," says Feet. "Now roll on a floured board." She snaps her fingers. "That's what I did wrong. Didn't flour the board."

By next morning-tea time she has a mound of scones she is satisfied with—clay coloured and a chef's-hat shape. Diced dates evenly studded through. She stacks a small pile on each of three plates, her Wedgwood serving plates, the ones with gold leaf edges. She covers them in tassel-fringed muslin and is ready for trip number one.

A quick examination of her appearance in the mirror first: is her hair sprayed high enough? Her face powder thick enough to blot out her cheeks' blemishing veins? Her frock, the yellow silk knee-length with peach and purple stripes and slashes. Two bracelets, one of rubies, the other her favourite, the chain of gold sovereigns that should give the ladies something to admire, she says, and keep the conversation going should it fizzle.

Trip number one will be to the neighbour immediately to the right of us, the one whose mailbox is so badly spattered in tyre mud there's hardly any name at all.

"Who knows what I'm in for?" she says with a festive squeal and a sing-songing, "Welcome to me. It's welcome to me."

She settles the three plates of scones on the car passenger seat and reminds herself how carefully she will have to drive to prevent them tipping. Not so easy given she is not too keen on driving, especially this Monaro tank of a thing The Duke brought from Sydney. While it may be ideal for pulling trailers and horse-floats, it's as heavy as a tug of war to work the steering. If you touch the accelerator with the merest toe-push, the damn thing takes off like a jet plane.

The colour is more to her liking. "You can certainly see us coming, I'll pay that," she chuckles. Silver with orange bonnet and boot, a combination The Duke calls sporty and Feet calls original.

As for that thump-thump grumble of the motor, she calls it a racket for all his calling it a V8.

She crosses the zebra-crossing of shadows and gives two goodbye hoots on the horn.

★

She gives no *I'm home* toots on her return a half hour later.

Trip number one came to nothing. "Not a soul at the next door's," she purses, pulling number one's scones from the seat, not caring that the top layer topples to the upholstery, to the car floor, to the grass. She snatches each back onto the plate and squashes them to "stay" as if punishing a pet. Squashes them harder as if hoping to hurt them though she can only make them crumble.

It is herself she means to punish. "That will teach you," she mutters, hardly parting her lips. "If you're so stupid to bother with bloody peasants like these, it's your own fault. No one to blame but yourself."

Then it's The Duke's turn to be punished. He is standing behind her smiling to receive the news of her outing, though his smile flags because Feet says as if accusing him, "If we're so stupid as to bother with peasants like these, it's our own fault."

Then to me, "That's the only word for it—stupid."

In the kitchen she empties the plate into the rubbish bin with a "Stupid. Stupid" as if berating the scones.

The Duke insists on being told what on earth has happened to put her in this foul mood. Feet breathes deeply that she does not want to talk about it. The Duke knows this means she does want to talk about it. She wants to talk about it very much, desperately. It's *all* she wants to talk about. But she intends to delay talking until he stops asking and she becomes resentful of not being asked. "Thanks for nothing," she will then say, bitterly. "Thanks for your interest. Or lack of it," she will add, sarcastically.

He has stopped asking and turned away from her towards the back door.

There's her "Thanks for nothing." Now her "Thanks for your interest. Or lack of it." Now her explanation for her foul mood can begin.

Trip number one may have been a non-event, but never mind, she simply moved on to number two—the Dutch mailbox called Van der something. She knocked and knocked. No answer. "But do they think I'm a complete dill? I could see someone moving behind the curtain."

She's damned if she's going to be standing at someone's door, knocking and knocking to give scones to people who haven't the common decency to open a door. "I made *that* clear to them, I can promise you that. I tore out of their drive like Stirling Moss." Feet nods a self-congratulatory smile and declares that she couldn't care less about types like that. Types who lurk behind curtains. "To hell with them," she says, snapping her fingers like a spell that sends people hellward.

The Duke puts his hand on her shoulder, kisses her temple and says it's not the end of the world. She pushes his hand away and tells him that if he's not interested in listening to her, if he has better things to do, then he should go and do them. "I wouldn't want to *keep* you," she says, sniffling and putting her knuckle to her bottom eyelid as if about to lose mascara with crying.

The Duke apologises if he misunderstood her. He thought she had reached the end of her story.

Feet's eyes widen angrily. "Did I say it was the end? Did I? What made you think it was the end?" Her voice has gone hoarse with containing herself.

"You snapped your fingers and I thought that's the end of the story."

"I haven't told you about trip number three."

"I'm sorry. I'm all ears."

"If you have got better things to do, it's no skin off my nose if you want to listen or not."

"I do want to listen."

"I really couldn't be bothered if you're not interested."

"I am interested."

She puts her knuckle to her eyelid again. She walks into the sunroom. The Duke follows to place his hands comfortingly on her shoulders but she waves that she doesn't want him to see her cry. He takes out his handkerchief and offers it, but No, she says, she has recovered now and somehow managed to keep the tears at bay.

Trip number three began promisingly enough, she says. It was the next driveway over from the curtain lurker, the one with the white goat chained at the gate the way some around here do for good luck. "Such a pretty goat, I thought to myself. It raised its head and made a baaing sound as if pleased to see me."

But the farmhouse itself was less than inviting, more a falling down cottage in need of bulldozing. There were happy dogs wagging their tails and tongues but there the welcome ended. "I knocked on the door, and who comes to greet me? The most sour-looking prune in a hair-net I have ever set eyes on. I said to her, 'How do you do? I thought I'd bring around some scones.' And do you know the extent of her conversation? I'll tell you—'Thank you.' Not so much as a 'Would you care to come in?' She took the scones, Wedgwood and all. Didn't empty them on to her own plate. Just closed the door."

Someone will have to go back and fetch her good plate. "That's a job for you, I think," she nods to me. For she, as she drove out of the hair-net's drive, promised herself never to set foot there again.

In fact never again will she be sociable like this. Not with these types with their lurking and their stealing her Wedgwood and closing doors in her face. "Where I come from you don't close doors in faces," she rasps like a warning, a threat. "Not in my face you don't."

She has begun to dig in her hair and mutter wet swearing. Spit bubbles at her mouth corners. "Bugger them. To hell with every bloody one."

★

But promises are only temporary. Especially, says Feet, when you are fortunate enough to have the kind of husband she has. Someone with the ability to put in a nutshell exactly how our neighbours must feel.

We must look at it from *their* point of view. "I should feel sympathy for them. Not anger," she says, shaking her head annoyed this never occurred to her. "Here we are with the best property in the district. And there they are just chipping away, chipping away, as they have always done in life."

Just imagine it, she laughs, her fingers resting below her throat. They must feel intimidated to see the lady of a showpiece like we have turn up on their doorstep out of the blue. "They'd take one look at me, and then one look at themselves and their mothy old cardigan and their grey hair that needs a good tinting and doing. Those horrible hormone chin-hairs they haven't plucked since God knows. Not to mention the state of their house. They probably haven't cleaned their house for an eternity. Too busy, or too hard up even to get a cleaner."

The Duke is emphatic, we really must try to fit in: "It wouldn't kill us to try that little bit harder because you never know when we'll want something from them. Even just paying their share of a new boundary fence. Even just the loan of machinery. We want to keep in good."

He puts the question to Feet: "What's the one thing every person has in common?"

She shrugs that there are so many things it's impossible to list them. Everybody wants to have nice clothes if they can afford them. Everyone likes to go out for dinner to somewhere swish.

"No, no, no." The Duke wipes his hand across his face. "*Family. Family.* That's what we all understand. Rich, poor, Chinaman, Jew. And that's how we should present ourselves to our neighbours. As a family. It shows we're just like them in that regard. That's the something that will break the ice."

★

She wishes she had done this in the first place.

A phone call only takes a minute, that's all it takes, and look what grief it saves. She claps her hands together at how wise a phone call can be. No one gets caught on the hop by having you turn up unannounced. There is time for them to clean. There is time for them to prepare refreshments, stock up on drink, have their hair done. "Would it be convenient if we popped over?" she said to Face-ache, and Face-ache said "Yes." Hesitated, it's true. Didn't jump for joy, but who ever jumps for joy to have people invite themselves over for afternoon tea?

At least our Face-ache had the good graces to say, "That would be nice," and suggested the occasion be held at the main house, her parents-in-laws', at 2pm tomorrow before the evening milking.

"Not the midget house, thank God. We'd hardly fit in," Feet quips with a laugh-grunt, her fingertips over her mouth as if she just belched.

A new batch of scones is called for.

And those fawn shoes—The Duke will have to take his fawn shoes from the wardrobe, the ones with the silver buckles, and rub away any black scuffs with soap and warm water.

She insists he wear his fawn suit to match. Not that she wants him to look too formal. But when worn with his white skivvy and red pocket handkerchief, he is the very essence of smart.

She herself is tossing up between her orange pantsuit with the matching string shoes, so cozily flat-heeled to spare her arches and corns. Or she could try the candy-pink jumpsuit with or without the yellow belt. Either way, she thinks it time to break out her necklaces. The pearls might be the thing. Or maybe just plain gold. "My lordship, what do you think?"

The Duke holds out his hands and pushes down on the air. "I think we shouldn't be going over there all flash and dolled up. We're not in Sydney now I remind you. I think we should play us down."

"But what's the point of having nice things if we don't show them off?" Feet states, not asks.

"I'm only telling you what I think. I don't intend arguing over the matter but I'm just saying I think we should play us down."

"Well I'm not going over there in gumboots, that's for sure." Feet stands square to him and puts her hands on her hips.

"No one's saying we're going in gumboots."

"That's a relief. But I'd still like you in your fawn suit if you don't mind. If it's not too much trouble."

"I'll wear the fawn suit. But I think you should go easy on the jewellery."

Feet sighs and promises to wear her polka-dot neck scarf instead. "Is that played down enough?"

"It's a start. I don't think it's too much trouble to put ourselves to if we want to fit in a bit more," The Duke says.

"Scones, polka-dots. I think I'm making every attempt possible to fit in. But one has standards. Why shouldn't the lady of Tudor Park wear jewellery? It might encourage a little more pride in other people and their presentation."

She goes to the kitchen to make more scones, talking to herself about how people should come up to *her* standards not the other way round. Not her come down to theirs. "That's all I can say. Them up. Not the other way round."

Mixing the dough, she talks to herself: "I am not about to compromise on standards, thank you very much."

Ironing The Duke's skivvy, his red pocket handkerchief that lends such a splash of colour to a man: "Your standards drop and you might as well say 'I've let myself go.'" Her voice register changes, lowered to a man's to mimic The Duke: "Fit in why don't you. Compromise your standards."

Then her own voice. "No thank you."

Then a rougher man's. "Come down to our standards."

Her own again. "Where I come from you bloody well work hard to get nice things and wear them."

On it goes this mumbled argument like a private parliament of herself.

★

But by 2pm next day she has talked herself into the view that wearing jewellery in the country is much too risky. A bracelet can become hooked on a branch. Try finding a sapphire in all that grass. Sydney has burglars and pickpockets. Here the culprit is long, thick grass.

Besides, if being a good neighbour is so important to her husband, then it becomes important to her. She understands perfectly how useful neighbours can be, especially with us away so much in Australia and staff running the place—reliable one minute but what about the next?

She ties her polka-dots around her neck like cloth jewellery. She tells me I needn't shave because my week's re-growth has barely sprouted. I may wear jeans on this occasion because it's a manly, countrified statement in the young.

Face-ache did tell Feet her name on the phone but now she has forgotten it and hopes she doesn't call her Face-ache out of habit. "What was her name again? I think it starts with a C. I've completely forgotten. Carol, Kate or Carly something." She pours herself a calming glass of riesling.

Why have I allowed Feet to speak to me in this way with her "You needn't shave" and "jeans on this occasion"? Why no farce of fury until The Duke restores the chain of command?

It is because I *do* want to make a manly statement with jeans in the country style. I have already checked for any sign of re-growth. Had there been whiskers on my cheeks and chin I would have watered the candle-flame and gripped the Safety in the limply way to respect my neighbours with a presentable face.

For I don't merely put my hands behind my back and walk with my twitch self to oversee Churchill. I don't merely cat's-cradle with Norman and son, perfecting my not-looking technique so they see that an education doesn't deprive a man of hardy pride. I also gaze in all four directions at this grass and milk civilisation. I bring it up close to me with a lend of The Duke's binoculars. There is blue sun on our mountains if a storm cloud covers it over. The milk tanker man puts his wireless to his ear and jigs while he milks the shed that milked the 500 deformed humans. I imagine I am duke of it all, the four directions, its commanding citizen. In time its mayor, its look-up-to man. Perhaps even one day, yes, its member of parliament.

History would happen to me in this place after all.

Such advancement would not be beyond The Duke were he a better-read man with a head for speeches. He's the *doer* kind—he has no time for fancy speeches.

What an achievement to crown his legacy I would be.

Today I am going to meet my constituents, my neighbours. Perhaps word has spread from Norman and William that I am highly qualified in mind, a person of learning, who is adapting well to their way of life—I am clearly someone not afraid of manual toil. "Look at his forearm scar, the O shape," they may have gossiped to others, having admired its purple blister.

I also have added some scars to my hands. Lifting hay bales by the raw twine without gloves burns and swells the fingers till there's blood. Bale prickles dot my knuckles and leave a puffy poison in the wounds. The blunt knife that cuts the hay twine also cuts well into skin. By using a chopping motion the rusty blade sinks where you aim it. Same with sharp rock—a chop, a grimace and the skunning's done.

When Feet and The Duke ask how I got these scars, I say from working. Plain hard work.

Perhaps word has spread already through Taonga that I am one of their people now, but obviously above them.

CHRISTINE, NOT CAROL, says Face-ache.

Her mouth is bent up uncomfortably in a smile. Her eyes shyly avoid ours.

Feet apologises and says she doesn't know where she got *Carol* from. "Wait a minute—yes I do. I was thinking of a woman I know in Sydney who is the spitting image of you."

The Duke and I glance at each other and arch eyebrows because this woman, this Christine, is like no friend of Feet's from Sydney. She has no peach-tinted or bleached salon-sculpted hair. Hers is brown with grey through it, cut below her ears like The Beatles. No make-up over the cracks and saggings of her face. Not a dab of red on her lips or fingers. Her clothes could be a man's—khaki trousers, blue pullover shedding dags of wool.

No woman in Feet's circle smells as Christine smells—stale milk. Not even fumes from Feet's perfume can cover the cow-shed taint in the air.

The Duke touches Feet in the small of her back, his signal for her not to talk too much, not to speak for the sake of speaking as she has just done.

Feet taps his fingers away irritably. She does this as Christine leads us down the hall where now there is a faint piss-stink in the air. Piss of soiled human not soil-animal.

The lounge contains shades rather than colours. Through the west window a see-through stream of sun flows, squirming with motes. On either side of the flow, dark armchairs and walls, a settee with crochet coverings.

Feet has her sneer-smile on. She uses it when something is not to her taste, a house like this for instance which she would call dowdy. The Duke steps behind her and places his hand on her elbow.

"Ah," she sneer-smiles. "Well, here we are." She presents Christine with scones folded in a swag of grease-proof paper tied with a blue ribbon bow: "My mother's secret formula." She pokes The Duke's arm for him to please pass Christine our gift of a bottle of champagne.

Christine blinks at the bottle with a sneer-smile of her own though she accepts the bottle politely enough, saying "You shouldn't have done that" as she takes it by the neck.

She turns to two men sitting on the other side of the sun stream. They stand, one very old, skinny, tanned, who steps momentarily into the stream. He has a bald head, white where a hat would normally be. The other man is a younger he, identical in face but with a pale hair-mist over his crown and more flesh to his body. They wear short khaki pants, no shoes, just socks, the ends of which flop the way socks do when boots have been levered off heel-to-toe.

Suddenly from a room down the hall, an old woman's ailing voice: "Who is it, dear?"

"It's the new neighbours," Christine replies and in the same breath introduces her father-in-law, Jim, and Jim junior, *her* Jim, her husband.

The Duke and I shake hands with the Jims. I offer a good grip, a three-second squeeze to make a manly impression.

The Duke has always advised that it's not a tussle of strength, nor is it a standover ritual. A handshake says: I look you in the eye and greet you forcefully without force. Unless, of course, your fellow shaker is an *opposing* shaker, a challenger attempting to assert superiority over you. That's when forcefulness is legitimate, as retaliation. Grip-pressure time may be extended in that circumstance well beyond three seconds to five seconds, seven, or even, if needed, nine.

On this occasion, shaking the Jims, I want to appear honoured to be in this house, their family home, the seat of who they are. I've decided I am especially honoured that they felt no need to dress up for our visit. They're content for us to see them as they live, in their natural state, their garb of every day.

Feet, still sneer-smiling, will consider it offensive, disrespectful. But I am willing to see it as the purest form of welcome.

Yet, as honoured as I am, I must not appear too honoured or obliged to them. My being here is as it should be.

This is only our first meeting but it's a chance for them to realise their future depends on me.

Squeezing their hands that reach out across the stream is not like squeezing human at all. More log of wood than skin and bone. Wood with rough, splintery bark. No pressure is returned by them in the finger and palm embrace.

Christine fans out her arms for us to sit. The Jims return to their side of the stream. We of Tudor Park stay on our side and sink between musty cushions.

"Who is it, dear?" the hall-voice inquires again.

"It's the new people," Christine answers, still not looking our way but pulling dags from her pullover, flitting from one section of the pullover to another. She informs us that the voice up the hall is her mother-in-law who is an invalid and frailer by the day.

Oh, we nod, sympathetically. There the conversation stalls. Stops. We sit in nodding silence.

★

Silence is for finding a way out of silence. Feet has deep breaths for trying to escape it. She crosses her right leg over her left, then changes to left over right and breathes heavily.

The Duke has his throat to clear. On this occasion he also has crochet arm-rests to pick and rub and admire.

The other side of the stream must be used to silence. The Jims sit motionless. One of them, I can't work out which, has a whistling block in his nose.

I would rather not waste time in silence. I want to know what subject brings these men alive. What would make them, ordinary people, but men of property at least, feel at ease and willing to confide in me as their future leading citizen?

That hall-voice again. "The Van Hoots, is it?"

"No, the new ones," Christine calls back.

A kettle puffs and squeals in the kitchen. Christine stands, stuffs a handful of dags in her pocket and asks, "Who has milk and sugar in their tea?"

"Oh, I see," Feet says with a small laugh, confused. "I'd said to myself, 'Champagne.' I just assumed. I'm sorry."

Christine picks off a dag and glances at the Jims. The Jims look at each other. They scratch their heads in identical timing and bite their lower lips as if confronted with a problem which must be solved this moment, now. Christine goes into the kitchen. The puff and squeal die away. She re-appears with the champagne.

The Duke leans over and whispers to Feet. She frowns and stares into the stream. Then, pressing her fingers to her throat as if to keep laughter down, says, "White with one, please." She lets up two sneering chuckles, the way she does when she's put out, cross. "I hope we haven't offended you by bringing alcohol into your house."

The Duke smiles across the stream to the Jims. "It probably wasn't appropriate."

Feet frowns an apology to the Jims. "My husband says this is a strong religious area—Brethren wasn't it? We just presumed that since this is a special occasion."

"We'll know for next time," The Duke declares.

The hall-voice this time is stronger, more insistent. "Who is it then?"

Christine ignores the question, puts the champagne bottle on the sideboard and goes into the kitchen.

That nodding silence again. Then Feet uncrosses her legs and says, "I admire people of religion. Not that I go for it myself. But my word, I've thought of starting a religion. What other business gets away with paying no taxes? Makes the lurks *we* can claim pale by comparison." She lets up a hearty laugh.

The Duke laughs with her but tries to catch her eye to hush her.

Jim senior leans forward. "We had a bottle of beer in the house once. But we gave it to Rosie."

Jim junior nods that he remembers.

"Rosie?" Feet inquires, pointing to the hall as if presuming the name belongs to the voice from down there.

"We drenched old Rosie with it to bring her gas up," says Jim junior.

"Goodness," Feet leans back, shocked.

"She had the bloat," says Jim senior.

Jim junior gets up from his armchair and takes a framed photograph from the mantelpiece. He steps through the stream to show us Rosie, a palomino-pale Jersey. "Super milker was Rosie." Another photograph. "This one here is her mother, Lil."

The Duke and Feet perform admiration with muttered Ohs and "My word."

This is the opportunity to display my scars and my new knowledge of Jerseys. If I take the photographs from Jim junior, make my movements very slow, leaning well forward into the sun stream, even my red prickle spots will be clearly in view.

That is exactly what I do. I reach out to take the photographs, and I'm in luck. Jim junior doesn't want to let either photograph out of his grasp. He actually hugs them away from me. My fingertips are allowed only to touch Lil's frame, which they do, my scars held up right under Jim junior's nose.

"I dip in iodophor. Is that what you do?" I blink at the two Jims, then blink downward so their eyes will follow mine to my scars for admiring the O shape and the white and purple infections.

Jim junior hasn't a clue what I'm directing him to do. I give him a hint. "Your Jerseys probably kick less than our lot. Jerseys are much better natured, don't you think?"

Jim senior nods, "Rosie was a gentleman."

The scars are not attracting the attention I expected. Yet, I should take that as a compliment. My scars are so convincing they are considered little more than part of the everyday way of things by these two men with splintery wood hands.

Feet wrinkles her brow and shifts to the edge of her chair for a closer inspection of my scars. "You must be very clumsy," she says.

I pull my hands back to my lap, my face suddenly so hot that surely it will split with blood rage.

I unclench my jaw enough to manage a sentence. "It's from hard work."

But Feet will not stop. "I know it is, dear. I'm just saying."

Clumsy. A word that applies to half-wits. Not a word for using about me in front of two experienced, hard-handed farm men.

Christine sets a tray down on the table by the settee.

Silence again. Filled with the chink and spoon-stirrings of tea poured from a large metal teapot and green cozy.

Now the whistling nose. Our swallowings make squelching sounds. Feet's hard scones crunch in our back teeth.

"Personally, I like them like this," she says. She lifts her cup and saucer high to read the maker's name underneath. "These are lovely cups of yours, Christine. Who made them?"

"They've been in the family for years," Christine shrugs.

Feet squints that no one appears to have made them going by the blank space where the maker's name should be. "I adore a good crockery set. I have Wedgwood, Royal Albert. You look at them and you sip and you feel like royalty."

That hall-woman again. "Who? Tell me? Who?"

"I said it's the new neighbours," Christine calls.

Half-wit. There is nothing remotely half-wit about me. What half-wit would ever know about the *other* Wedgwood? Does Feet know? Does The Duke? The Jims? I'm no half-wit. I know that Rosie and Lil made it into those frames because of Thomas Wedgwood. And I say as much: "Thomas Wedgwood had the brains to discover that silver salts darken in sunlight. From that we got photography."

"That's nice," says Feet as if apologising for me. "But let's not get too deep."

This time the hall-voice is cracking with strain. "New neighbours? From over the road?

"Yes," Christine replies wearily.

"You don't mean that fancy pants tart, do you?"

Feet is motionless mid-sip, the cup rim between her lips.

The Duke has just returned his cup to the saucer. His finger does not unpinch from the cup's ear. He doesn't swallow his mouthful immediately. He waits for Feet to swallow first.

Her throat finally squelches down her sip. Slowly she places her cup and saucer on the table.

Christine peers down at the floor. She picks a dag. Another and another. "Poor old thing she is. She's not what she was," she explains.

"Indeed," Feet says quietly, her mouth going into its pursing position.

The Duke wonders, as cheerily as he can pretend, if that Thomas Wedgwood I mentioned is directly related to the crockery Wedgwood. "You'd think so with a name like that, wouldn't you?" he asks of all the room and offers up his palms as if we might place our answers there.

I tell him that yes, I'm sure they are related. The two Jims nod indifferently.

Feet purses, "Indeed, it must be nice to have a talented family. Never mind. We can't have everything."

She is digging her nails into the upholstery, so deeply the red of them disappears in the folds. If she were standing she would be close to her two steps one way, two steps the other way stage. The Duke has read the signs too. He sits up straight, slaps his hands onto his thighs and says we mustn't hold these good people up any further—milking-time must be getting near. "Yes it must," he confirms from his watch.

"Indeed. We best be going I think," Feet digs, and stands, and is already walking along the hall before The Duke and I have finished handshaking the Jims and Christine.

The Duke says he is delighted to have finally met some of his neighbours. He hopes they have a good milking season and make plenty of money.

I add my thank-you for showing me their photographs.

The Duke says that when you're new to a place it's a boon if you meet people you can rely on to help you out once in a while. And vice versa, of course. He says it's lovely to have a good old-fashioned cup of tea with neighbours, and he hopes we can do it again.

"Amen," I say. Devout types like these will appreciate an Amen from a younger man. An Amen makes you seem plainer as a person. My scarred hands are their kind of hands, they'll be thinking. That and his Amen—he is just like us.

★

Feet is already in the passenger seat of the Monaro, window wound up, rear-vision mirror twisted her way for any lost lipstick, for any make-up smudges or flakings.

As soon as The Duke slides into place behind the steering wheel she starts: "I'll give them *fancy pants tart*. Who the hell do they think they are! Bastards with their cups of shitty tea. As if I'd be interested in photos of bloody cows. Invite people around and that's all you get. Too lazy to even put on a pair of shoes. They make me sick, the bastards, the lazy pricks. I've got a good mind to go back and get my champagne and they can stick their *fancy pants tart* up their arse."

The Duke tells her to quieten down unless she wants them to hear but Feet says she couldn't care less if they hear. Let them hear. They're *nothing* to her.

The Duke reminds her that we invited ourselves into their house, and in that case we have to take what we get.

Feet snorts her contempt for such a notion. "Be on their side if you want. If that's the way you feel. To hell with you too. I can't bear it. Sell bloody shitting Tudor Park is what we should do. Or burn it to the ground, the lot of it, every blade of grass. To hell with it all."

The Duke brakes the car with a gravel-skid. "Go back and get it then," he yells, thumping his palms on the steering wheel. "You want your champagne then go and get it for Christ's sake."

Feet sucks in a seething breath. "Don't you talk to me like that. Drive the car. Get me out of here."

"You're full of hooey."

"How dare you. I have to get out of this car this minute," Feet seethes, head in hand.

"Well get out."

"And let *them* see me, the bastard shits with their spying eyes? See me thrown out of our family car like common filth and made to walk home? Oh Christ, what have you done to me? You've lowered me to this, this mixing with cow people. Get me out of here. Get me out of this shit bastard place."

IT HAS BEEN four hours. Four hours, and the second self has not returned her safely from the ghost train.

She curses and digs, grabs her hair and curses but has not arrived home up her rattly vertebrae to her washed and whistling mind.

We call and call, The Duke and I. He that it's getting well on into the evening and we should have a meal and play Euchre perhaps, the three of us, for something to do, and she can be the dealer to start with. And even though we should be four not three to play it properly, it passes away the time with its trump plays and left bowers.

Impossible, Feet digs: how can she be expected to play a silly game when those bastards over there are laughing at her with their *fancy pants tart* talk and *her* bottle of champagne they're probably feeding to a cow.

I call to her that I walked down the road and retrieved her Wedgwood plate from the woman in a hair-net. I lie that the hair-net woman praised her scones and admired them being presented on such a lavish dish.

Feet seizes the plate from me. Holds it up for inspection.

She finds a flaw immediately. "There!" she gasps. "The bitch has ruined my Wedgwood. Shitting bitch like all the other bastards. She's cracked my beautiful, beautiful Wedgwood."

No she hasn't, The Duke says, inspecting the plate under a light.

No she hasn't, I agree with my eyes that are young. Reliable younger eyes.

But her eyes are all that matter. What do *our* eyes know about her beautiful Wedgwood? *Her* eyes see a crack and that crack means *our* eyes are just trick eyes deliberately not seeing cracks in order to drive her mad and stick horrible, hateful pins into her. "I'm not fooled by your trick eyes."

She stomps to the kitchen door, out through the fly-screen and flings the plate to the concrete. It cracks open down the middle, surrounded by the shattered white and gold shards of its edges.

In she comes through the fly-screen to fetch the broom and rubbish bin. She is muttering through a slit in her lips, words of no clear sentence for understanding.

Out she goes and sweeps the clacking pieces. "My parents wanted more for their daughter than this, sweeping up Wedgwood because of cow people and snide hatred from shits who spy and call me names."

The Duke steps onto the concrete to say, "Let me do that" and "You go pour yourself a wine" and "You go lie yourself down."

But Feet holds the broom at arm's length from him so she cannot be accused of shirking her duties, of not keeping this ugly little farm cottage clean like women should. *Her* instincts always told her to marry into money but no, she had to fall in love instead and start with nothing and work to get ahead. For what? For name-calling shits and bitches who defile her possessions.

She sweeps and mutters to the concrete. "I've tried to remain an attractive woman but I can see I needn't of bothered. Who'd want *him* now! Ears tucked up in his silly bloody cap. His underpants poking over his belt. Who would want him! I should have let myself go and had him divorce me. At least I'd have money instead of filthy cattle."

The Duke raises his voice and points angrily. "You just shut up. You're not Greta Garbo anymore yourself."

"I won't be told to shut up by you. *You*, who if you'd had any gumption would have made us oil millionaires many times over."

The Duke swats the air to signal he is not going to listen to her anymore because she's just a typical woman who loves to make a scene and isn't satisfied unless regretting something and being bitter.

He says to me, "Women love these games and arguments."

Feet sweeps the concrete so hard the pile of swept crockery is re-scattered. "Gumption," she says, spit spraying from her lips. "He didn't have the gumption," she wants me to know.

The Duke sits on the back step to pull on his gumboots and tells me not to bother with her.

But *she* tells me not to bother with him. She says that all it would have taken was a bit of gumption and instead of buying Tudor Park we could have bought an oil well for a song. An oil well that as we speak is making millions for some other man because that man had the gumption to be the winning bidder. "Imagine the life. We'd be building a house not here but smack dab on Sydney Harbour. Invitations to all the best dinners in Australia. It doesn't bear thinking about. 'Oh yes, we're in the oil business,' we'd be able to say. Instead of 'milk.' Hardly has the same ring."

Oil? Never have I been so proud of The Duke. My own father was going to be an oil millionaire. This man of mine with his tucked-in ears and Jockey underwear always showing. His greying fuzz of hair. This uneducated doer, one who came from nothing but has built himself a legacy for his son to prize.

"We could have owned oil wells?" I ask him, awed.

"Perhaps," he says with a groan of not wanting to discuss the matter.

But buying oil wells is not a subject to be mentioned and in the next minute forgotten. "Where were the oil wells? Why didn't we buy them?"

The Duke doesn't reply. If he was merely remaining silent out of modesty, I would leave questioning for another time. But his silence is a frowning, uncomfortable, hiding-something silence.

Feet answers, "In Western Australia. An acquaintance of your father, one of his horse-racing contacts, was starting up an oil company and invited him to bid to be a partner."

"Why didn't we do it?"

Feet sighs, "Gumption."

The Duke stands, stamps his gumboots into place.

"Can we still buy them?" I ask, excitedly. "Can we change our mind?"

"No," says The Duke sharply. He raises his voice to Feet to remind her that he knows nothing about the oil business, and even if he could change his mind he wouldn't because the oil business is out of his league. "It's the big time."

I step away from him. He has shocked me. He has disgusted me with his "out of my league" talk. Talk he would call *defeatist* in me. The talk of a weak man, a disappointed man. A Gunna.

He moves towards me, but I don't want him close at this moment. I certainly don't want his hand to touch my shoulder. I see him extending his arm but I take a step away.

He says, "We can only go so far in a lifetime." His voice is soft, no, it is weak. The weak voice of a disappointed man with no gumption. "Perhaps with your education you'll get your own turn to do such things and you'll be able to say 'Yes Sir, that's for me.'"

"When would I get that opportunity? You just passed up the perfect opportunity," I say as disrespectfully as possible by closing my eyes, shaking my head and slapping my palm against my forehead. My father has let me down and now I have deformed humans instead of oil for my legacy. Norman and son instead of blackened men in hard hats on great steel rigs, drilling into the earth to fuel the world. How could I ever have been proud of this defeatist? I can't look him in the face. And because he has let me down this way I feel justified in calling him a Gunna. Which I do: "You're a Gunna."

I still can't bear to look at him. Let him be offended. Let him be angry. His son is telling him he's a Gunna. And I'll tell him again if he disputes it.

"You make your own way in life then. *You* do better. You go out and work at your own thing, you ungrateful, spoilt little ..." He doesn't finish the sentence.

Now I look at him. His chin is quivering with rage, no, with holding back tears. Tears pool at the bottom of his eyes. He quivers to Feet: "What kind of ungrateful bloody son have you bred?"

Feet lets the broom handle drop. She begins to quiver back at him. "I've done my best. I'm sorry, but I've done my best. If my best isn't good enough, then I'm sorry."

I say to The Duke. "I thought you were building a legacy for me. That's what you told me. Now you tell me to make my own way. To go out and work at something else."

Feet begins her pacing right to left, right to left. But instead of digging into her scalp and boiling spit in her lip corners, she kneels and weeps. "I'm sorry. I'm so sorry." Tearless crying at first, but then The Duke goes to her, kneels, hugs her and says that he is the one who should be sorry. Sorry for saying she had bred such a son, such a terrible thing for him to say. Tears drip from her, spotting the grey ground.

Feet tells him she's sorry for saying such hurtful things. For raising the oil-well nonsense and getting so worked up as she's given to do.

I have no legacy now? Am I on my own?

I probably went too far calling The Duke a Gunna. He has after all provided Tudor Park. It could be worse. He could have nothing.

Fortunately I've learnt a trick or two from Feet in my sixteen years. I know how to get my legacy back. "All right, I'll go out and work," I announce. "I will leave school and I will get a job and work. You want me to make my own way in the world, well if that's the way you feel, that's what I'll do. I don't want your legacy."

The Duke shakes his head that he doesn't like hearing me talk about leaving school and not wanting his legacy. Feet is sobbing against his chest and he winks that he needs to comfort her.

"I want to leave now. Right this minute," I purse. "That's what *you* want, so I might as well leave."

There, that's brought him from Feet. Even so, just to be sure, I walk away from him.

He follows: "I don't want you to leave. I'm building this place up for you. One day it will be yours. I want you to have it."

"I don't want it."

"Please don't say that. This is all for you."

Feet's crying becomes louder. Her I'm sorrys more sniffly and shrill.

But I haven't finished with The Duke. I hunch my shoulders and pretend to cry. And pretending causes my eyes to wetten. I can now turn to him and look at him with truly wet eyes. "You say I should go out and work. But I *do* work. Look at my hands. They're all scarred from working for you. This O shape one, it makes me sick it's so painful."

The tears and the talk of sick puts me in such a swoon that I begin to sway, collapsing. The Duke steps in to hold me and take my weight and says how proud he is of me for working so hard. We'll put some Dettol on that cut right away because I'm precious, I'm his boy and with us as a team Tudor Park will be a showpiece. Us as a team will be his life's joy.

WHEN I FLY, the pilots are pleased for me to visit and stand behind them. They are important men. I gape at their dashboard of instruments. I admire their white shirts and name-badges. They are like doctors of the air world. Their dials, switches, valves and buttons are the wind's gauges, the sun's vital signs, preparing a medical report of sky-blue health, the fits of turbulence, the off-colour clouds of storm.

They turn around in their dashboard chairs to look at me, narrow moustaches like an eyebrow over their smiles.

But on this trip back to Sydney there is a difference. When they extend their hands for shaking I notice their arms are tanned from sitting so much in front of the sun. It is not work to sit in front of the sun. Their tan might as well be a beach browning. Their tan is not from stepping out of milking-shed shade to slap cows into the jaggings. It's not from lifting new-made rectangles of hay from paddock to truck. The green twine that binds the hay blistering the fingers so that they bleed water.

Nor is there sweat showing through the doctor-pilot's underarms and collar. Is it work to *sit*? Can these two things, work and sitting, be done together? And to wear a uniform. A uniform as schoolboys wear uniforms.

I've begun to think as an employer of men thinks. I would not employ these men on my Tudor Park, so neat and clean, thin-armed from no toiling. How could they touch the privates of cows? They are too educated for cow touching. They would always be thinking they could have done better in life. How could they be a Norman, Bill or Jim?

I'm certain they smell the cowness on me. They did not rise in their seats to greet me, formally, as an equal. Don't pilots usually do that with me? Yes, I'm sure of it. I'm sure they used to.

A hostess brings them coffee. They sip and wince at the brown heat. Or is it a smirk they're suppressing that makes them close one eye and blow? A pulled face of how I'm not one of them. I am from a place called Tudor Park, a toucher of cow parts, a mere man of the land for all my being an heir.

I must not become too educated or I might want to leave Tudor Park. I might learn too far beyond it. I would become like those pilots for whom the very air is not nature but maths on a screen. I would make my own way in the world, turn away from my legacy and break my father The Duke's heart.

★

In Sydney a real doctor with stethoscope for a necktie. Cold hands and questions. "This wound," he asks of my bandaged O shape. "It's a stubborn little healer. How did you do it again?" He peels the gauze back to its antiseptic slime.

I proudly say a cow. The hoof of an angry cow.

And how long ago was that?

Over a month.

And does it hurt?

Only when he squeezes it and a yellow dot of pus pops out.

I ask him how many times a day he washes those hands of his to make them so unnaturally cleaned of all contact with the world. I mean the question as a sneer, an insult that a man should have such sterile-pink fingers.

He answers "plenty" with a long exhaling, wise and weary. He asks if I have taken the bandage off, against orders; if I have played sport with the O bared to the elements because how else could grains of dirt deposit in the O's edges? He's going to have to call Feet from the waiting room. He can't have me ignoring explicit instructions not to remove the covering and thereby waste his professional time. "Don't you want this to get better?" He asks this in a tone I don't like. It's an admonishment for one. But is it also clever prying? Whether by accident or science he has asked a question I answer yes to when I mean no.

★

But I don't have much dirt left. I filled three jars from Tudor Park before we left—from the paddocks closest to the stables: two small Vegemite and a large one of Vicks. I scrubbed them out with iodophor for the black soil of my legacy, the moist earth of me with its lace of grass roots and brook that trickles underfoot when you walk it.

I rub it on me, press it under my nails like dry soap, an unwashing. I lick my tongue onto the soil for its metal-blood taste, and always keep a few pinches folded in my handkerchief for emergency unwashing if my hating the city becomes too much, its harbour seeming hideous, the useless slow-coach yachts like proud flags of leisure and laziness.

The beaches too, where people get out of their real beds only to go back to bed in sand. They buy ice-cream. Do they know where the cream came from? Do they know that someone was up at five in the morning to get it from cows? Do they know that tonight's steak comes out of the ground, from grass that passes through the cows until the cows are then put down and cut into pieces? Do they know that cows are just deformed humans and so we are really eating ourselves?

Shakespeare said all the world's a stage. He must have known that this is the cow's revenge, this process, this great cycle of birth and death on a stage like Tudor Park. He must have known that the most important of all places is a farm. Not a church. Not a parliament, a court, an office or school or hospital. But the farm that puts food in your mouth. That milks a cow or kills it. And all the while, what is happening to you? Your hours are ticking away too. All the Tudor Parks of the world are feeding you up for slaughter by disease or accident or old age.

★

When the O started to heal I rubbed the soil in. The first rawness of the wound came back to me, red and lumpy.

I don't bathe anymore. In the evening at shower time I don't stand under the water. I birdbath between my legs and my underarms if Feet complains I give off smells. When I shave once a week I use The Duke's electric razor not the candle-flame.

I keep soil smeared under my shirt, my socks. I squeeze a tennis ball to build the muscles of my hands, to swell them oversized like a mitt. I expect it will take years of this for them to be like Norman's.

At The Mansions I keep my hands especially grimed. When The Citys remark on the state of them, I say it's due to work, real work that you can't wash out so easily as their fathers can with their doctor scrubbing, or the big-wig ink from their barrister fountain pens that soap and water rubs away.

The Scrubbers return from holidays with similar dirty nails and work wounds to me. But theirs fade. Why don't mine? they ask. I reply that where I come from soil doesn't fade. It is so strong and fertile a mix that it leaves a lasts-forever stain.

"Liar," they call me. "You're no farmer. You're City. My old man says no 300 acres ever made a dollar as an enterprise."

★

I calculated the soil would last three months, till next term's holiday when I would return to Tudor Park.

But there is bad news. We will be staying here in Sydney next break, and the one after too. The new Tudor Park house is being built and Feet has no intention of inhabiting rooms without a roof. What civilised person would live with no toilet connected, no kitchen stove, no nothing! We are certainly not going to pitch a tent or hire a caravan. That would really get the binocular people looking down their noses: "There goes fancy pants tart. Reduced to living like a gypsy."

We'll remain in Sydney until the new house is livable and beautiful and it's *we* who do the looking down our noses, and do it from a second storey which means *they* have to look up at us.

What's more, it's one worry off her mind to know I'm out of the clutches of the town's available girls. "Oh wouldn't they love to get their hands on you. You'd be a prized catch, mark my words," she says, lowering her puckered mouth to kiss the wine glass's lip for as long as it takes to sip.

A prized catch indeed, she repeats, and she is not talking about whether I'm handsome or not, or wide-shouldered and tall and speak well. She is not talking about whether I have a brain between my ears. Those attributes I possess in spades, she says. I inherited well from her. Even though country life has coarsened me, compromised my hygiene and given me a rough, arms-out, monkey-male walk, it cannot kill off her genes in me. No, what she is talking about is the subject of money. "I can just see it," she sneers. "They'll start sniffing around. They'll start throwing themselves at you with their big udder breasts. And suddenly there you are at sixteen with a little bastard baby. Oh yes, the little sluts would be set for life is what they'd be scheming."

But no one was sniffing around, I say. Feet kisses up a mouthful of wine and gulps it quickly in order to speak. "Not yet maybe. But one minute you start shaving regularly and the next you start having urges. And because all men are weak and all females conniving, there you would be at sixteen with a bastard baby. And there I'd be with a daughter-in-law like those pram-pushers at the corner store. It would kill me." She closes her eyes and shudders what she calls "the shudder of the dead" where someone has walked over her grave. "Me a grandmother, at *my* age. I have no intention of aging any further at present. I have no intention of wearing the grandmother label."

She says she's going to leave The Duke and me alone. She wants him to have a good man-to-man talk to me. "I'll leave you two to it," she says, leaving the room and closing the hallway door behind her. Just before the door clicks shut she says, "Men. Weak, weak, weak. Little sluts would tie you round their little fingers."

The Duke wants me to sit on the sofa and listen to him. "She's right, your mother," he says. "You've got to be careful, a boy like you with his life ahead of him and a Tudor Park to think of, and girls who might want to trap you by using that thing between your legs. That thing between your legs can get you in trouble. Is that clear to you?"

Yes, I nod.

He slaps me on the knee and winks. He stands and takes a deep breath of satisfaction, of a matter having been settled and solved.

He stares through our balcony's sliding glass doors. Our apartment is three levels up above the park called Rosa Gully in Vaucluse. We can see north to the Diamond Bay cliff face and the shabby brown flats perched on it that Feet says shouldn't be allowed to claim the postcode. The Duke likes to stand as he is now and admire the ocean below that sends a spray to our faces. The way it turns from the deepest green to white bits and pieces in this weather! The wind may make the sliding doors rattle through the night and would keep the dead awake but when you have the sun on full beam and those bits and pieces flickering away it's a thrilling sight to see.

He puts his fists on his hips to survey the sea before him as if the proud owner of it, the duke of the waters off Rosa

Gully. And all the yachts that sail there only sail with his permission. All the fish must trespass out of sight below the surface. His sea, his non-land, no soil, no grass. There is no work to do with it but stand, fist-on-hips and watch water.

I stand beside him in the same pose. I breathe that it is quite a sight.

The Duke leans towards me. "That thing between your legs is how a girl says *Gotcha*. Understand?"

Yes, I understand.

"Think with *this*." He points to his head. "Not with *that*," he winks and points down to my groin.

I will, I will, I say. A whine of embarrassment in my voice.

The hall door opens. Feet is clipping her earring to her left lobe because that lobe will have been pressed to the door for listening. "It's all very well saying *I will, I will* as if you're being put upon. You haven't stood in that corner store buying sugar. You haven't suffered mothers of those pram-pusher types asking bold as brass if my son has a beau. 'He's a good-looking boy that son of yours. Has he got a girlfriend? Is he spoken for?' One hideous cretin with a bum like a sack of porridge wanted you to go to her daughter's birthday. I told her 'No thank you, he's busy learning his father's business.' I told her you've got a lovely girlfriend in Sydney, just to throw all them off the scent. See how your mother looks after you? I'm prepared to lie through my teeth to protect you."

If only arranged marriages were an accepted practice to this day. Her mind would be more at ease then, she says. "I'd soon weed out the gold-diggers. *I* should be the one who decides these matters. I should choose who succeeds me as the lady of Tudor Park. But no, it will be left to a boy and his urges. And then the little slut leaves him and claims half of what is ours, us, mine."

THERE WAS ONE.

I have kept her as a secret until now. I must collect more secrets because secrets are mine, a thing *I* own.

But how could she, that skinny Bettina, think I would bother with her ilk? Her father's holding is only a third the size of ours. It is close enough to Tudor Park for him to be classed a neighbour, and he was neighbourly in his offer to help make this year's hay. But in return for what? For nothing? He could think of no favour The Duke and I might do in return?

"This is my daughter," he said to us. "She brings good sandwiches. She can also drive a truck. She has plenty of grunt for lifting any bale size."

The audacity to think *she* would ever catch my eye, her oily brown hair parted on the side like a man's. Man-tall, surely six foot if an inch and her shoulders slumped forward to try and hide it, which made her chest mounds sag beneath her T-shirt.

She left school at fifteen—what had she done the year since? Cooking and cleaning around the house like another wife for her father.

She ran beside the truck, matching me lifted bale for lifted bale. She threw bales around without gloves or any hay-wad padding between the twine and her fingers. She barely spoke, just smiled.

When we broke for lunch at midday, she served me salad sandwiches, served them with a little speech: "I made them myself. Hope you like them." The gap between her front teeth showed pink gum and grey fillings.

Next day she served biscuits she called Dutch Bakes. The lemonade was also hers—her aunty's recipe, her mother's lemons. I squeezed prickles from my knuckle skin. She offered to cycle home for tweezers to extract them properly.

Then in one shy sentence she said my shoulders were the widest she'd ever seen. She made a mixture—castor oil and vinegar—for rubbing to stop them sun-burning.

She asked to be my pen-pal. I almost gave her my Sydney address. "I've never written to Australia before," she said.

To think I would want to read a sentence of hers! Fifteen and left school. She would hardly know five verbs. I would feel duty bound to correct her spelling; send her mail back with many red cross-outs. I could give her marks from one to ten and say, "Stick to making sandwiches. Write back when you get an education."

I deliberately told her the wrong number for my street—it was the safe thing to do.

But then I told the correct one. Why? Because she flattered me, she complimented my singing. I am so weak I give way to one flattering remark.

Singing is easy. It is exaggerated talking. I try to do it under my breath which keeps the melody vibrating in my throat, around my teeth, cheek-bones, gums, rather than be emptied straight out of me by singing loudly. It used to be my secret, this singing, but the very act of singing lets the secret out. Someone overhears you. Feet overhears you and then you might as well shout.

Other people try a tune with nasally, off-key embarrassment. But *I* can sing to Elvis Presley and mimic his voice exactly. Same for Tony Bennett, and Louis Armstrong and his gravel-growl. The ones Feet called The Oldies, playing her 45s when drink dances in her.

I can croon, but I can also reach Robert Plant's high, hard-rock screaming. I have the cockney "only" down perfect in David Bowie's *Sorrow*. And Bettina had an ear for it if there was little more to like in her.

"How can you sing while lifting hay? You must be so fit," she admired, and asked if it was *Green Green Grass of Home* I was singing. If so, it sounded just like Tom Jones. She said she'd never known someone who sings as I do, in tune, not amateur, but a real voice like the radio.

This kind of comparing I accept with a thank-you, a puffed chest of pride, a closed-mouth smile that acknowledges the compliment but expresses how well aware I am of this, my talent for songs.

Other comparing I despise. I would never allow a girl to compare me to other males, as males compare females to females. How one's breath reeks like off meat. One's cunt smells too fishy. One has too hairy a crack but her father runs Treasury. One is too intelligent, another is not intelligent at all. On and on it goes.

Boys are told not to hit women because men are stronger and gentlemen moral. But a girl who compared me to other boys—how do I get revenge? I would want to harm the other boy if he was compared to me more favourably. I would want his more handsome face made uglier. His carved muscles crippled in him. His sharper brain damaged to dullness. His richer family made to live hand to mouth.

Has Bettina compared me with another? Some *catch* she has had her eye on from the local batch of farmers, truck drivers, shop keepers, nobodies? What is she thinking to herself about me these two months on? Is she giggling to a friend that I can sing and am an heir at least, but my ears are pointy wings? I'm so weak that a girl like her can match my bale lifts? My legs are so thin, mere sticks when the wind blows my trouser-legs around them?

If so, then she should know this: I think of how her sister delivered fresh sandwiches one evening. Her younger sister by at least a year, and pregnant and sweating from her bulging belly. But with thicker, shinier hair than Bettina.

It flicked around her face in a breeze, stuck in the corners of her lips so that she had to hook it free with her finger. So much prettier, with a white gapless smile and copper skin. Forearms without blemishes of moles and dark hairs. No wonder she was already taken. I should say as much in a letter to Bettina. I could make her bawl with jealousy— her own sister her rival. Her sister took my eye more than her even though she was claimed by another man's seed. *That* would punish her for giggling about me or comparing me to others if that's what she has done. And if she has done that, it is typical of the children they call girls.

She should know this: I am too old for her. Not old in years, but in the rest of me. It is my most savoured secret: I have kissed a woman. A full-grown woman not a child, but someone forty. Her name was Genevieve. At night, before sleep, I play with myself to her memory. Not just the memory of the kiss itself. Of having the breath of another in my mouth. The smoke-wine tang of being entered by her spit, her breath and tongue. Nor what followed on from kissing—the fingering into one another's clothes to our most private skin. Her jerky sob-sighing that surely was bliss, though it could have been misery for the sameness of the sounds. No, not just that, but the transgression: my lust is no normal lust. It prefers a face lined with laughs and frowns of the years, webs of eye wrinkles and shoulders sun-freckled, cleavage cracked with aging. I learned this because of Genevieve. My lust prefers the powders and perfumes applied to cover these shortcomings which are not shortcomings for me, but safe-signs. Arms hanging off the bone, soft and with a rubbery feel to the touch, yet not under-swaying as fat people's do.

When Genevieve walked, her breasts quivered at the seam—a safe-sign. The child-girl Bettina's breasts were male-hard as muscle when she stood up straight.

Genevieve's voice was not a screech-girl's, but a cigarette rasp. Genevieve would never giggle about me or compare me to others. I was her secret too. I was her taboo. She was a friend of Feet's transgressing with her son, a lad, a mere fifteen.

What would farm girl Bettina say about that? People like me live by different rules. We take the day off school to go to parties at Melbourne Cup time. Proper parties with adults and gin, society people, Sydney faces from TV. We flirt with a Genevieve while our parents are in the other room. Never mind that her own son is at the same school as me. Never mind that her breasts are breasts *he* would have suckled, the bastard son of a judge and Genevieve the judge's mistress. Genevieve called me hand-some and swept my face and arm with her long, sharp fingers. Stared straight into my eyes and held the look like a dare.

Dear Bettina,

People like me use our father's cologne and shave for the benefit of a Genevieve not a plain, farm female like you. No unsightly hair must repel her. No whisker-prickle when she sweeps her fingers. People like me write poems for her. People like me return her lingering looks and stares. When the Melbourne Cup is playing in the lounge we two close the door into the laundry and kiss proper kisses, feel to those places only lovers can see bared.

Of course I will never send this letter. I protect my secrets. And what would Bettina write back if I did? That people like me are disgusting? How dirty to be mixing with a woman like that, a female almost three times my age? How dreadful to be taken advantage of in that way?

Dear Bettina,

You are so innocent, naïve. What was dreadful is that it only happened once. I thought my sweet Genevieve had felt pleasure, but suddenly there were tears. She pushed away from me seconds after our first kiss and feel. No more linger-looks ever followed. No more hand-sweeps or skin-touch. No "We must do this later," no "Skip a class at school and come here."

I rang her but she wouldn't speak to me. I knocked, but only head-shakes from her. She held her hand up and said, "Please. It's crazy. Please go." Said "Goodbye" very curtly and closed the door.

"Can't we have Genevieve to dinner?"

"She's gone. Greener pastures I suppose," said Feet. "Gone to Surfers, and not so much as a courtesy cheerio."

Bettina has not written to me as she said she wanted. I will never waste my time pretending to write to her again. Even one letter from her—was that too much bother? She must have compared me with someone and judged that *they* were the better.

A gold-digger, that's all she was. I must live more by my wits. Types like her and people like me must never mix our genes.

I CAN SING.

They can't, The Citys and Scrubbers at The Mansions.
I laugh to hear them try. And why do they try? Because I
goad them, the rowers and rugby players with their weight-
lifter thighs, a plump *y* of muscle parting over their knees—
strutters and jostlers in their teasing play-fights of
camaraderie. Or strumming their sides in a guitar memory
of the latest Double J record.

But watch their cockiness turn to shy when I say, "Go
on. Sing it." Usually *they* cause jealousy in others, but now
it's them who feel it; and feel it for *me*. "If you like music so
much, then sing it," I say. "If you think Bowie is a star above
stars. If you think Robert Plant is God's voice and Alice
Cooper's a demon, and Springsteen is nature's blast of aveng-
ing horns, then don't you wish you could make the sounds
yourselves? Go on, try it. Sing. *I* can. Listen to me."

Friday assembly-singing. All boys must stand for a half-
hour's session to "oxygen" our brains and learn the disci-
pline of chorus, the art of voices joining. We must respect
these songs we sing, the war songs of our forefathers, men

who fell so we could live in peace and freedom. Songs that saw them through the hell of battle, death by Nazis, invasion from the north by cruel, fanatical Japanese. Songs that cheered men and so should cheer their descendants, dressed as we are each Friday in boy-soldier uniforms for parade. The blue cadet airforce and white navy. Kilt and brown army shirt for diggers—a belt whose brass must shine like silver. Red flashings for our sock elastics, trimmed to a frayless upside-down V.

Sing the legacy of sacrifice of saving us from evil.

Bless them all, the long and the short and the tall. Pack up your troubles in your old kit bag and smile, smile, smile. Keep the home fires burning. On the road to Mandalay where the flying fishes play.

Sing *God Save the Queen*, no longer our national anthem but our racial one. The inheritance of a Crown that figureheads our history—the parliament we go by; the law that governs our liberty. Our manners; our deferring to the royal rank that rules us, a rank decreed by none other than God.

But why bother, I want to know? Why bother with a God who would give such a high rank as *royal* to someone other than me? History and the Commonwealth are the Queen's Tudor Park. And to her I am a second-class citizen like any other citizen, condemned to live out my days resentful and respectful that I do not myself hold that God-granted rank. What reason is there for striving, for living at all, if not to believe I was selected by God for special deeds?

Not a slave to this world. If not an equal of God then at least his favourite among the lesser.

Let the Queen come to my Tudor Park when I inherit it. There I would be her King. There *she* can sing God Save *me*.

★

There is no God, they say.

But if there is, if "No God" is wrong, he is responsible for my voice and at Thursday morning chapel I am prepared to sing to his name for that small favour that singles me out among others. Sing not to praise him like a supplicant grovelling for some titbit of good fortune, but to flaunt my vocal jewellery, flash it against the stained glass for his attention.

The jealous strutters mumble-sing the hymns, but I blare. *Oh, God our help in ages past, our hope in years to come. Our shelter from the stormy blast and our eternal home.*

The Reverend looks up from his hymn book. Why such disapproval on his face? In me he has a singer. It is hardly a shame to have a voice that outshines the rest. Let boys in the pews snigger that my effort and talent are being treated as misbehaviour. They're too embarrassed to sing these songs that are not rock songs but the thees and thines of poetry they despise.

It wouldn't take much to turn their sniggers to laughter-howls. God's attention is not a rapt attention. He has no

need of singing, hymns or prayers. His is a silent watching
if anything, nothing more. If God exists, he is someplace
far off like a distant parent, not close like Feet and The
Duke, but distant with too many children to ever keep track
of them and no longer any care to. But the boy-eyes around
me stare white-wide in anticipation of my next loud, trill-
ing hymn.

I want something new to impress them. They won't
expect Blake's dark satanic mills, his arrow of desire, in the
manner of Dean Martin: I swallow the words into my throat
to be trapped there at the back of my tongue for lazy vibrato.
A drunk-like slurring and dying fall to the last long word
of the first verse.

They would not expect Tom Jones for the second verse.
His animal gasp and growl. An aggressive emphasis on
every U-vowel, a hoarse I-vowel, a pleading E. Easy from
there to slip into Engelbert Humperdinck's nasally drawl
with lips almost shut to affect a complaining strain in the
melody.

The Reverend looks up, mouthing the hymn in his
distraction. He doesn't need to scan the chapel for the
offending singer. He must know it's me. Who else can sing
so beautifully, so cleverly in another singer's shell! I hold
the hymn book way out in front of my stomach as if short-
sighted, an elegant theatrical pose. I switch from one
mimicked voice to another without submitting to grin-
laughing as those around me are.

I end the hymn as Louis Armstrong.

Whenever IOUs appear in the passed-around plate there is an interruption to the service. We are interrogated by the Reverend's pointed finger—"Was it you? Who was it? You? Or You?" When a boy confesses, he is made to stand and be noticed, singled out for mass shaming. He must walk down the aisle and be seen for what he is—a debaser of God's house.

I've considered confessing even though I have never put an IOU in the plate. I have no great wish to insult the poor. But to be marched down that aisle to the pulpit, one boy out of one hundred, standing, walking, all eyes upon me, famous for that moment to the hundred in that chapel. Fearless to approach the Reverend, his fingers twitching from rage. The twitching spreading through the tips of his robe. His black hair coming loose across his forehead. Me walking with jauntiness in my step. My teeth clenched to square my jaw. I draw my top lip down in a pouting grin as if to say, "Come on then, get it over with. I'm bored having to wait for you to grab my suit-coat sleeve and lead me like a horse across the garden, onto the quadrangle where more boy-eyes can witness my fame."

I will be held in awe, whispered about: "What's he done? What's happened?" One brave applauder will say, "He must have IOU'd the plate."

Still jaunty when we reach the staff room, I'll be instructed to wait outside in the corridor with its notice-board announcing the First XI for Saturday. A row of trophy cabinets. Honour boards—captains of rugby teams, tennis, school captain, duxes. My name will never appear there.

Now the Reverend with his cane. He will have selected a thin one. He will flick it through the air: "This should drive out your disgracefulness and let in some shame."

I have been caned many times at The Mansions. For smoking, for what they call an "insolent air." But a maximum of four cuts, not six. Six is the punishment for chapel IOUs. Even so, I would still bend to touch my toes as ordered with the nonchalance of doing exercise. I am no Poached Eye. I won't shake and shiver, frightened. Not me. "Where I come from we work around them, not through them," I would say to the Reverend, and take the six strikes with barely a grimace—my O shape caused me more pain; lifting hay bales without gloves and padding.

And when the caning is over I would walk, no, I would stroll, smirking, saying, "Thanks to you, Sir," meant as a mocking. Stroll without giving in to touching my behind to soothe-rub it. There will be no tears from me. I have proven many times over I can be composed after four strikes. Six is only two more.

What awaits me in the quadrangle will be worth the extra aching, the searing burn reaching deep into my groin, my anus. In the quadrangle *they* will be there to welcome me as a hero: boy-eyes, hundreds of them. Hands slapping my shoulder because I have lasted six cuts of the cane and look at me—no hint of suffering.

I will have broken the ultimate rule at The Mansions: always yield. Always. Always. Be subordinate to the ones with *master* titles who, after they punish you, look for it in you—that you've been buckled by them and now have a broken will.

By the time I sit in class there will be blisters weeping sticky fluid into my trousers. The doctors' sons among us will say, "Come on home with me this arvo after school. Let my dad attend to you."

The lawyers' sons will insist their fathers take my case and have me sue. And I will believe they mean every word of it. "Thank you," I will say. "I'll do as you advise." My new friends and admirers who want me, this famous boy, as theirs, though I am not usually one to like, so aloof, so angry-proud. Not from professional lines—just a no-name family, but accepted as one of them now.

Of course, by the time the bell rings to go home, their fathers, as it happens, will not be able see me: "I forgot my dad's busy with surgery all week." "My father's doing a murder trial. He won't get home from court till late." I will take what they say as truth, at least to their faces, though I know it is really friendship cooling. Friendship that never got warm.

Let my singing earn me six cuts, ten, or even more. Call me up the front and punish me, Reverend. Make me the famous among my not-friends.

Instead, he takes the lectern. No punishment. He speaks

of Jesus being inside us like a green seed that is growing to choke out the dark weeds called sinning.

I will sing louder next time. He will have to act against me. My not-friends are expecting it.

FEET CAN PLAY two tunes on the piano—Remembrance and Robin's Return. The three Rs she calls them. She spreads her fingers above the keys, pushes down, closing her eyes to recall the gist of the opening bars. The opening bars of each song are all she has ever been able to play, taught to her as a girl by her mother. "My mother could play those songs right through—such talent." And given that it's forty years on, what talent she herself must have to be playing a tune's gist from memory.

The brown upright piano in the corner was bought for my benefit, it disappoints her to say. An attempt to make me the life of any *do* and have the air of a little bit arty. But what did I do? Wasted it. What a hit I would be with my clever way of singing if I tickle the ivories as well.

Now salt-spray has glued the internals so the ivories stick. There it stands, its only friend is Mr Sheen. A constant reminder to her that young people want everything too easy these days. If they can't play a tune automatically, they whine that it will take years to practise. "That's an attitude you never inherited from me. It must be your father's side. But that voice of yours, your way with a song—my musical gifts have obviously been passed on."

The Duke reminds her that his father could belt out a tune on the piano. Jazz of all things. But he was too drunk ever to take it further. "I've always hated the sound of a piano because of his bang, bang, banging, playing drunk after pub-time," he says, pointing to our piano as if levelling an accusation. "He should have provided for his family instead of all his bang, banging. He had whisky. We had mouldy bread."

"Well we have fresh bread now," Feet says impatiently. "Frankly I resent the notion that a drunken barber would have contributed to our son's talent, if that's what you're suggesting."

"What's wrong with barbers? *Your* family were butchers. Is that better than barbers?" he says sarcastically, raising his voice.

Feet refuses to have a depressing conversation involving butchers and barbers. "Butchers and barbers—why don't you yell it out louder! Why don't you tell half of Vaucluse our every secret!"

She curses that he has such a typical man's fog-horn voice, but at least she has an antidote to it in mine. "Sing *He'll Have to Go* as Jim Reeves. Please do. It sends me," she swoons and says *Please* again. Please let her have one pleasure in life. She can't bear to go *out* anymore. *Out* means there'll be people, and people equal snide. If cow people spy and laugh at her and name-call, what are real people out there in Sydney doing? "I can't face them. Wouldn't waste my time with them. Shit bastards, all of them. Bastard bloody rude."

She leans back into cushions, her right leg stretched straight along the suede tan sofa. Her white sandal dangling from her toes. A cool breath has risen from the ocean and puffed the balcony drapes open. Feet pulls the hem of her orange house-coat up over her ankles, her shins, over her knees. It lets out a static crackle. She lifts the house-coat higher so the air can blow breeze between her legs. She scratches at a hot spot on her calf where a blue worm of vein has buckled into a varicose sore.

Put your sweet lips a little closer to the phone.

Let's pretend that we're together all alone.

She lights a cigarette and takes a long kiss of her wine, her head swaying as she swallows. Her foot follows the rhythm of my singing. Her sandal drops to the carpet.

I'll tell the man to turn the jukebox way down low,

and you can tell your friend there with you he'll have to go.

Why does it send her so, this song of men competing for a woman? Or,

Please release me let me go, for I don't love you anymore,

To waste our lives would be a sin. Release me and let me love

again.

Does she want that for herself, The Duke gone, a new man for suitors, lovers?

"Sing it holding my hand," she asks. "Sing into my eyes. Kneel down. Sing it like you mean it from your heart."

I tell her I'm doing my best. But the very act of saying that breaks the spell for her. "You're quite hopeless. You'd think it wouldn't be much to ask, a little song that makes me feel womany again and the kind who can still turn heads, who could walk down the street and attract 'Oooos.'"

Sometimes I deliberately sing off key for a few notes and it frees me for days from her wanting to risk another broken swooning.

Just a Closer Walk with Thee, sung with the Ray Charles negro rasp. That sends her too, though Jesus is there in the verses. Does she imagine Jesus loves more than just her spirit, or would do given the chance? She sway-sighs as if he is the ultimate catch to have.

★

I only need to hear them once and my body moulds me to the song. My tongue and throat match the singer's sound to my own, narrowing the airways for correct pitch and drone. An automatic process I hone by listening to the 45s on the lounge-room gramophone. I copy their manner too once I've seen them on TV.

With Nat King Cole the smile is so splayed my lip-corners ache, but the effect of such relentless happiness is to strain the voice so it rises into my nose. From there it is trapped, released and swallowed back down into myself with Cole's tender vibrato fade.

Jim Reeves is a deep moan, soft, sweet to the ear but if I toss my head whimsically with every word I lengthen the phrasing, stretch each note more darkly.

These are not songs for someone my age. What more proof do I need that I am old, not in years, not fully in body, but in those other ways: the way I accept my duties as heir to Tudor Park so good-naturedly, enthusiastic. I'm responsible before my time.

Old too in the way I know that safe-signs are found in women, not in girls.

Women listen to the old songs. I should have sung for Genevieve.

I fall to pieces, each time I see you again.

I fall to pieces. How could I just be your friend?

My Jim Reeves would have prised opened her door. Would have swooned her inside to her lounge, her body holding my body, her bed taking me in.

Where will I find a replacement?

At the races with The Duke. Putting my arm around the waist of the girlies in the Members Bar. Girlies, not girls. Girlies of the flirting men, string dresses low-slung so their skin is more obviously seen and offered. They look children alongside the ugly men who rub hands in their back's hollow, grandfather-old with leers white as dentures and shirt ends bulging loose over their belly belts. But they are safe-sign women to me—over thirty, armpits beginning to wrinkle and dimple at the sides; the first cheek-veins appearing, powder holes of open pores. Freckled shoulders from so much tanning, but not yet sagged to a crack between their shoulder blades.

I have watched The Duke do it himself, whispering, smiling close to their hair. Closer still when that hair is hooked behind the ear like a forefinger invitation. Taking care to place his hand only lightly against their hip when ordering a drink. Removing the hand when the drink is ordered. A polite moment of keeping his hand away, then placing it back and leaving it there if the girlie approves by moving more his way.

How disgusted I've been to see him like that. Him thinking with that thing between his legs, as he tells me not to. I felt ashamed, betrayed, brooding for Feet's sake that his hands touch hollows other than hers.

But there has been no "Gotcha" from a girlie to take him away from us. Feet has her song-swoons of other men. I've had my safe-sign Genevieve and no blame for the lechery.

If the girlies let those old men touch them, then a younger man, a me, would meet much more welcomed surrender. The Duke's copper-brown suit fits me, the one that goes shiny in sunshine and is made of such cloth that to sit down leaves no creases. The legs are a half-inch shorter on me than him, but I have brown socks to bridge the distance. My black school shoes, nugget-scrubbed are fine.

Cream shirt, blue-dotted tie from The Duke's tie drawer. Not his hair oil for my side-part, but a dry, natural flick-away style.

While he is leaning over the birdcage rail. While he is matching race-book names to parading horses, I will light a cigarette. I will order a drink, a whisky and soda or a seven-ounce beer. The barmen are like bookmakers: they know to serve me without questioning my age. A near-man in a good suit is a full man at the races.

I rehearse my next day at the races. "Excuse me Love," I say. The *love* said roughly and manly in the manner you speak to girlies, so they know their place as a girlie. "Buy you something? Champagne? Something queer, a cocktail?"

I will then put money on the bar before she has had time to answer. I do not look in her eyes until I have glanced the length of her—toenails, legs, hips. Never breasts until last. I then say, "That dress, it's very fetching."

But I have no money. Ten dollars only from the last Doncaster meeting. The Duke knows the winners. He has contacts. He knows the losers. He knows the favourite which someone somewhere says must "bomb." By Race Three ten dollars can make fifty. That's more drinks than I need for twenty girlies.

"What do you do?" she will ask.

Student. No—some prize I would seem. "I am heir to Tudor Park, my family's rural interests. Hence these old scars of mine."

She will feel my hands. She'll say, "Hard hands, a soft heart."

*

Feet has towels to fade and so has no time for races. Even though The Duke has his new horse, Bazza, racing. Even though the big fellow should run the Randwick mile out well today. She no longer can be bothered with friends. "When you're young, you don't see it," she says. "But when you get a bit of age on you see your glamour's gone out the door. No one wants people to feast their eyes on that and risk comments."

Instead she must follow the sun around the balcony for hours, keeping the clothes-horse of towels in front of shadows. When the towels' blues and pinks have paled from three weeks' washes and sunshine—wash, sun, wash and more sun—she returns them to the department store to complain they've lost their colour. "It says in the guarantee, if they fade within the first three months of use then the company will replace them," she tells the assistant, and points to what she calls "the literature." She says she has only used them a handful of times and barely washed them and yet all the colour has bled out. It's disappointing to spend good money on products that simply fade.

The assistant presents her with a new set and apologises for the bad batch and bother.

Another shop, another set of towels. And sheets sometimes, their pretty, bright flowers mere ghosts of when she first bought them.

On arriving home she toasts her triumph. She clinks glasses with The Duke and jigs, "I'm very proud of my little system."

What system? I ask. Why do towels need a system?

Feet sip-kisses her glass and wonders why, if I'm at all smart I haven't worked it out for myself. Or indeed, didn't come up with the system my smart self. "Nice towels are, let's say, $10 each. If we buy them, get two months' use. Then three weeks of intensive fading on the balcony. Voila! We get fresh, brand-new ones, free of charge."

But why do that, I want to know. "Do we need to—are we poor?"

We're certainly not poor, Feet laughs. But of course she'd deny it. "Protect the boy," The Duke would say. "Financial strife would worry him sick and make his father a failure in his eyes. Not only have I failed him with oil in Western Australia, I have failed him in a worse way now. We are poor and his legacy is gone."

★

My lunches make sense suddenly. Cheese and jam sandwiches, though I can't bear to taste them. No lunch money for me like The Mansions boys have money. Cheese and jam. That way I'll learn the value of a dollar, and not slip into spendthrift ways. Because where we come from the world's not a restaurant. You eat what you're given. I too must inherit that age-old code.

But I'd rather starve than eat them, cheese and jam. And I do starve—I don't need food. How can I have an appetite when The Mansions awaits me each day!

Mornings are spent in sickness. I dry-retch at the thought of eating breakfast. On the mornings I shave, I wish I could shave away the parts of me I despise. As whiskers glide clean, if only the ugly blood-blue mole on my cheek would glide clean too. I dig the blade in to make it bleed, but still that mark of a mole remains. My nose, that bulbous thing the strutters call "pus-bag." My huge ears they pull as "aeroplanes." Did Genevieve suddenly realise she couldn't bear the sight of me, I was too repulsive and hideous a thing?

If I could rip the ears from my head with the razor, there would be one flaw less to tease, though my skinniness will stay, worse each week now the hunger pains don't matter. I could feed myself up but that would require eating, and I would want to vomit the food up until I was empty again.

I spend my days on guard against the strutters. My best chance is my swagger—hands behind back, the Tudor Park pose, as if I am too good for them. This nose is no pus-bag, it is a proud, hawk nose. These ears are wonders of Magi-made construction.

I must not play kick-and-run—I am not feared enough to repel beatings. Like Churchill I would fail to show who's boss among us. So, swagger. Swagger. Even when the deputy principal finds my lunches rotted in my locker: "We've had complaints—the smell. Please open up your locker and let us explore." Even then, my hawk nose is lifted proud-high. Every sandwich bag glued together, months of them, furred black with mould.

I pinch them between my forefinger and thumb. I drop them in the rubbish, one hand behind my back. Drop them daintily as sugar lumps into tea. My lips bitten together in a fake smile that I hope gives me a nonchalant air.

"Why store them if you had no intention of eating them? You're a strange one," the deputy principal sniffs and steps away from the bin's reek.

Strutters gather behind the deputy. They make the loony sign at me—a finger circling their temples.

I don't know why I have let this rotting happen in my locker. Feet made them, these sandwiches. I could not throw away the food of my mother. But I could never confess such weakness, such regard for the handiwork of a mother. Better to lie, and do so hawk-proud, judgmental. A lie that has claws, that is wise and constant as the moon. "I did not want to be wasteful, Sir. To throw out food when half the world is in famine would disgust me. I know the value of a dollar."

"You're a strange one."

"Thank you, Sir."

★

Yes, it makes sense now. We are poor. I can stand it no longer. It's time to hold The Duke accountable. "How could you let this happen?" I stamp at him.

"I've done no such thing," he retaliates with a frowning, offended stare.

I will not be protected like a child from the truth. "Then why are we fading towels? Why shift the clothes-horse so it follows the sun?"

"Because," The Duke sighs, "it's your mother's little thing. She has notions. And there's no way you'll ever get them out."

"What *little thing*? What notions?" It's low of him to use her for his lies.

"She gets notions in her head."

"What notions?" I go into the lounge and insist on being told by Feet herself to expose him. "What notions?"

Feet flares, launching herself from her cushions to jab out her cigarette. "I've got no notions in my head." She pokes the air with telling off The Duke. With the other hand she grinds the cigarette into the ashtray, her new ashtray from the knick-knack shop in Coogee, green opals she regrets are wasted on ash when you could hang it on your wall for its colour tones. "You should be saying 'Good on you. Well done for thinking up the scheme.' Someone else is welcome to if they have the brains. If a company is so stupid as to leave a loophole in the guarantee, then it serves them right to have me use it." She pokes again at The Duke. "You want your son to grow up and not use the world to his advantage? *Notions in my head.* That's the thanks I get for having initiative."

She bites on a fresh cigarette and lights it with an angry scratching of a match. She keeps the cigarette bitten in her teeth behind smoke-swirl while she mutters, "Towels. Damn bastard bloody towels. Shit bastard things. Things we bloody well dry our privates with. Bloody cheek to ask money for the bastard things, for something we dirty with our bodies and then just hang there on a rail for everyone to see. Makes me sick. I wouldn't waste my time with you both. You make me sick the lot of you. Sick."

She spits smoke with every word as if the second self has come this time burning language.

THE DUKE SMILES that his suit fits me better than it does him.

He puts his arm over my shoulder as we walk. He steps in front of me to inspect my presentation one more time before we reach the Members enclosure. He whistles a tune of his own random making, straightens and tightens my tie so it more gaplessly meets the throat. He draws the lapels together across my front and tells me, "Only do up the middle button because the middle button is the fashionable approach." He calls me a chip off the old block and pinches the prow of his blue pork-pie so the hat is as off-centre as is dashing. He pinches the brim downward to firm the fit on his head. Before he lets his hands fall to his sides he slides his thumb along the brim. Not to wipe something away but with a finishing flick as if saluting me.

He tugs his pocket handkerchief up into yellow dog-ears pricked upon his chest. He tugs mine too and reminds me to take out the handkerchief regularly through the day and fold two ends of it inward and one end down so I have two handkerchief ears showing not a crowded three.

Two stay pricked longer if you remember to perform the re-folds. "Maroon was an excellent choice," he says of my handkerchief selected from his drawer. "My congratulations. You're a chip off the old block with this style lark. Maroon goes with copper as does yellow with my blue."

He compliments me on my polished shoes which he calls mirrors, and can't believe I was a squirt in short pants just yesterday, or so it seems, and today I'm as tall as him or taller. If Bazza wins today, he'll appoint me his official lucky charm because what a day it will be—just we two together. Two men. Father and son as one.

He moves his binoculars down to his bare wrist from where it has been slung on his forearm. That way their weight won't leave an impression on his sleeve. Time to get going, according to his watch. First race will almost be closed for betting.

★

Ten paces and he shakes a hand. Twelve paces, another hand. Eight, another. Fifteen. Ten. Like a welcome dance where men exchange partners with each other, those they call Bob and Mate and Bluey. Passing on to the next hand in the crosscurrent of the crowd, saying, "Good to see you. Good luck to you today."

They stand tie to tie, hush-voiced after the initial cheerfulness. They lean close as if about to kiss, and whisper "The word is" and the name of a horse marked for "just going round" or "jumping out of its skin" or "probably needs the run."

"This is my son," The Duke introduces. Now it's my turn to dance, to take hands in mine, hands with gold and tiny gems on their little fingers. If the shaker is too weak a squeezer, I'm free to say so to The Duke when I've fared that shaker cheerio because he never trusts such people who have the grip of a boneless fish: "A spineless grip means they're spineless in reality, and liars."

Bart Cummings' hand passes as a shaker of firm hold. "You've met my son, Bart," The Duke says, touching my elbow to raise my hand and grip the grip of his horse trainer. "Training Bazza for me is as good as training for this boy," he says and winks at me.

Now The Duke nods "Neville" to the Premier and insists I nod hello to him as well though I see the Premier blink bewildered at The Duke who continues with "Good to see you again" as if they are acquaintances, more so, friends.

The Duke nudges me to look over there: "That Malcolm Fraser's a tall fellow, isn't he? Good thing too. You want a Prime Minister taller than everyone else I always think. It's commanding." He nudges me again with his elbow. "Would you like to meet him?"

I shake my head, No.

"Don't you want to meet the Prime Minister of Australia?"

"Do you know him?"

"I might," The Duke says, winking.

"Do you really?" I am awed that he knows the Prime Minister of Australia. And I am ashamed of myself for being awed. As if The Duke, my father, would not as a matter of course know the Prime Minister.

The Duke puts his hands in his pockets and shrugs. "I wouldn't say I know him." Then he grins. "But maybe he should know me. Ay?" He waves for me to follow him.

He skips into a brisk walk to catch up to the Prime Minister. He calls his name, "Mal," and reaches out to shake hands. The Prime Minister shakes but doesn't look at The Duke. He keeps walking on, a brown-suited tower-man— The Duke's hat barely comes level with his shoulder.

The Duke doesn't release his hand grip. The Prime Minister is forced to slow, to stop, to listen. "This is my son, Prime Minister." He clasps the Prime Minister's wrist for him to join his hand to mine.

Why would I want to meet someone who makes The Duke lower in rank, lesser in my eye? I cannot bear to look at this brown tower. I do not look at him as I shake, therefore he is disqualified from my life, he isn't even here with his hand around my hand.

But The Duke will not be quiet. He steps close to the tower as if to speak confidentially. He places a hand on the high brown shoulder. "I'll tell you this, Mal. Wouldn't surprise me one bit if this boy of mine is Prime Minister himself some day. What with his education and his leadership qualities. Mark my words, I've seen it for myself, he's a born leader this one."

The tower mumbles "Is that so?" and tries to walk off but The Duke has reached out his hand again for a parting shake and wink and nodded Goodbye. We watch the tower walk off through other be-suited winkers and nodders whose hand the Prime Minister takes without stilling from his stride.

"There you go," The Duke nudges. "When you get home you can tell your mother your old man introduced you to the Prime Minister." He puts one hand in his pocket and rocks heel to toe while gripping his lapel with his binocular hand as if in weighty contemplation.

★

The Members bar has a tide that goes out and comes in. A men-tide dictated by the loud-speaker din: "Horses are parading for the next race on the card. Riding changes—K. Moses for R. Quinton on number six."

When the tide is out men lean on the white birdcage rail, cheeks red from sun and drink. Race books hang open like a little wing span. They study the loping machinery of horses. Peering for flaws, for an imperfect setting to the pink breathing, the legs' cog rhythm. Skin must be tight scrim that shows compression of the ribs heaving, veins visibly threaded like electrical wiring. When jockeys mount, the settings must start speeding, the cogs bounce and spring as if combusting.

The tide-men crane and cup an ear for a trainer's confident whisper. They bet their fancy across the way with the bookmakers. They climb to the stands and watch with binocular eyes. They barrack throwing their hands forward as if themselves attached to reins. The process takes twenty minutes, then the tide returns casting ticket litter before it.

Meanwhile, the women remain on the islands of stools and beer-sticky tables. Some are wives, others girlies. Wives wear more jewellery than the girlies, their fingers are racks for rings, wrists for gold bracelets, bangles. Their hair is shorter and stiffened in circles and swirls. Many are attractive with my safe-signs. But many are too ugly in their saggings for me to offer them a wine. Their husbands—would they harm me if I tried?

Most girlies have no safe-signs at first glance. They have no obvious sagging. Their hair is still long. Their breast-line still above their ribs. Their backs have a goose-skin tan. You must get close up to see the masks they make with their make-up. The lip-corner crackings, and cracks around the eyes. Skin pores becoming too open. But even the oldest would be better than the youngest ones—eighteen, twenty—who would compare me, I'm sure of it, like girls of my own age. They're too close to being children to do otherwise. Yet, no matter how big *their* noses and their ears, to the bulge-belly men they are beautiful, adorable. Just as to girlies at the safe-sign stage—the Genevieve stage—my revolting features will be handsome as a movie-perfect face.

They, the safe-sign girlies, will have apartments to take me to; cars to get us there. If they are regular girlies for just one man, there are hotels with penthouse bedrooms instead of risking being caught in their homes.

I will have to buy them dinner. Drinks, a show of flowers. It's the third race now. I have twenty dollars from one winner and place.

At The Mansions the English text has been *Catcher in the Rye.* In it Holden Caulfield hires an older woman, yet he didn't want sex with her though she was a prostitute and wouldn't have cared. A book about people being phony that's fake itself, a lie! What boy-lust ever reasoned his penis down except in books? What boy-lust ever had a woman pull her dress over her head and is too depressed like Holden Caulfield for more than a bit of talk?

★

The Duke has no time for drinks or girlies today. He has a horse running. He prefers to stand beside the stall for an hour and say "Good boy" in worried ownership. He'll postpone his harmless flirting, his keeping his eye in, till after the race. Winning puts a gleam of smugness in his flirting eye; the swagger of riches in his step.

He likes first-time girlies—they're not wise as yet to his game.

"You've not been to the races before?" he'll smile. "There's a first time for everything. Let me buy you a champers and bid you welcome."

He'll introduce himself as proprietor of agricultural interests overseas. "There's money in commodities. Yes, they're doing all right by me." Then, "I'm owner of Bazza—my little extravagance. Not that I can't afford it. We should have the best in life if we have the means." And when he's had his pleasure of breathing them in, of placing his palm on their hip, then arm around their waist, then their arm threaded on his as if for chaperoning support, he will suddenly look at his watch. "Well, I best be getting home. My wife will wonder what's become of me. She would throttle me to see me enjoy myself."

The girlie will unthread her arm, step away from him, a scowl-smile of embarrassment, of having wasted time on him. She will glance at his left hand where he never wears a ring and say, "That's tricking not to warn a girl."

I light a cigarette and squint through the shield the smoke protects me with. I am not alone and shy with a cigarette and its smoke-shield. I have an action to perform, the action of smoking, sucking, sighing, locking my jaw to mouth a smoke of Os. I come with clouds between me and others. I am aloof but have companionship: I am the friend of a cigarette. I look older with him than with him not in hand.

I buy a glass of beer. Beer looks a real drink to be holding. Whisky and soda could be ginger ale to a watcher.

THE MEN-TIDE IS going out. I am to be left the only man
with girlies and their safe-signs. I have twenty minutes.
I must look their way and use my eyes to invite talk. I
have learnt by noting The Duke that a man does not
stand about, paralysed by fear. A man cannot stand about
and be attractive to a woman. He cannot sip his beer and
be manly. He must gulp it and sigh his satisfaction with
each mouthful. He mustn't fidget with his cigarette, con-
cealed in smoke. His confidence must cause him to bound
when in motion, to rub his hands together in excited
expectation, cock his head to one side and take charge.
This way the girlie has no chance to refuse. His "What
can I get you?" will be answered with an impressed
"Champagne."

I must pick one out. Attract her eye. *There's* one—over
there. Choose her. Dark haired. Of safe-sign age.

My chest thuds. It beats the breathing from me. My legs
falter, powerless at the knees. Far too weak for walking.

Two there are laughing. Are they laughing at me? They
are definitely laughing. It must be me. I am certain it's

me. They are not safe-sign girlies. No saggings, face-cracking anywhere. They are in their children-twenties. I have no doubt about those two—they aim their laughs at me.

No, they haven't even looked at me. I'm not the only figure of fun in the world. Others have noses, ears. Those two laughers, cacklers, how would they like it if I laughed at *them* in front of other girlies? In front of the men-tide when it comes in: "*You* have noses too, hooked and bent, a revolting pair. *You* have ears big enough to wrap an anchor round!" I will spit in their faces. I will stab a cigarette in every part of me I hate. Starting with my head and stab downwards from there, arms, groin, thighs. Let them laugh then as my flesh hisses with pink holes.

"Are you all right?" A woman, a woman-girlie. Hair black and flared to the shoulder. Skin tanned so deep dark her freckles seem to blend. Cleavage that bears the beginnings of a V-branch crack in the soft. "You look angry standing over here. Is something wrong?" Her teeth are dark too—white enough as teeth go, but with stain between them. Her voice has the smoker's thin gurgle.

"I was just thinking," I reply, shocked to have company, this company, a safe-sign girlie. "I'm sorry."

"Sorry for what? For thinking?"

"For disturbing you."

"You weren't. You looked scary, angry. Or not well, like a seizure."

She is laughing, but not in *that* way, the cacklers' child-girl fashion. She is amused and intrigued. It is in her voice—a voice gentle as affection.

Yes, I was thinking, I tell her. Thinking that I have a horse running today and it is a nerve-wracking business. But where I come from we don't bother with nerves because we have so many responsibilities, my family and me. What with owning an agricultural enterprise overseas.

"Tudor Park. You've probably heard of it."

No, she hasn't, she says.

I tell her she will do because I intend to be mayor of the district one day, its political chief. A word-gush that makes her stare at my mouth as if my talk has become visible. She is smiling. "That's impressive." She touches my forearm and says, "You're a card."

I flick my cigarette into an ashtray. Take out another. Offer her one. She accepts. "Madeleine." No prompting. She simply leans to my light and puffs "Madeleine." And then, "You're young to have so much on your plate."

"I'm not that young." I puff a cloud to cover my too-boyish face. I gulp the beer followed by an "ahhhh" exhalation and belch into my closed mouth.

The tide is coming in. Madeleine glances at it then back at me. She turns to go but stops and smiles a thank-you for the cigarette and says I am going to get very lonely standing here all day by myself. "You ought to mingle more."

I tell her I have just been speaking to the Prime Minister and the Premier. In fact I'm waiting for the Prime Minister to join me any moment.

"Oh." She arches her pencil eyebrows. "Goodness. I better leave you to it." She drifts with the tide.

And what will happen when no Prime Minister appears? Stupid. Better to have said I know no one. She might have stayed sympathetically at my side.

★

My beer glass is empty. My cigarette has burned down to near smokelessness, hardly any company to deflect being in this bar alone.

Madeleine befriends no one belly-man for long. A group of the older tide, wrinkled and bald, vie for her attention by interrupting each other's sentences in good cheer with "Oh don't listen to him" and "He's a notorious liar." Child-girlies already have a toucher of their own. Their bare skin stroked where the dress leaves their back exposed. Those touchers are the younger-old. It is Madeleine who does the touching in her arc of antique men: shirt cuff touching, shoulder; fingertips pressed to the tongue of a tie.

I order whisky and soda, leaning one elbow on the bar. I say the "whisky and soda" loud enough that Madeleine might hear me now that I stand close behind her. I don't say please with the order because it has a weakening effect on a man's bearing. Madeleine looks over her shoulder to me. I lift my finger to acknowledge her. I gulp the whisky, the fire taken out of it by the soda and ice. It allows for three gulps before my throat scorches. Another three gulps and it's time to order again. Another cigarette for a cloud mask. Then at last the loudspeaker calls out the tide.

It is so easy to be at ease. Whisky is the master of it. It says, "Follow me into the mist." Not the mist for hiding in that smoke conjures, but the mist of all the world's warmth and good intentions. I am the world's centre in that mist. I am the world's most perfect man.

Madeleine is coming my way. "Now you've got a happy look. Not a care at all. Quite a turn-around," she says.

"Yes," I laugh. I cannot stop the laugh. It's as if my laughter is outside of me, independent and free-willed.

"You've been on the happy juice."

It takes me two goes to pronounce, "Want some?" There is a need to talk loudly now because the loudspeaker is calling out a race from its perch in the sky.

"Your Prime Minister friend doesn't seem to have shown up. Just as well given the present state of you. You should sip not slurp if it's whisky in that glass." She takes the glass from me and sniffs it. She pulls a face and places the glass on the bar.

In this mist there is no affliction of fear. I can lean back on the bar and say, "Buy you one?" Again taking two goes. I can hold up a money note and not look at what amount it is—amounts are all paltry to me. I can wave the note around and not care that I drop it.

Madeleine picks it up. "Sweetie, you should pace yourself. Are you sure you're old enough for drinking whisky anyway?"

I stand stiffly at attention to display offence at the question. But my feet are too heavy for standing at attention. They stomp rather than stand. I tip to one side. My elbow tries for a purchase on the bar but slides. The whole of me slides onto my rear. I scramble back up with Madeleine helping. Behind her a girlie giggles, "Who's he?"

"Some political guy or heir or something," Madeleine answers.

The giggle continues. It is a safe-sign girlie—those sagging, deep smile cracklings. A safe-sign girlie is betraying me with the giggle of a child-girl. There is an intense prickling of heat around my eyes. I am in a trance of deadening tiredness, of entering sleep. I am being handled on to a stool and told "to sit there, Sweetie. Sit there."

★

The Duke demands that I walk. "Embarrassment. That's what you are."

He insists I walk and not lean on him for balance. Walk all the way out of here, out of the Members bar. Off the course to the carpark. I'm to concentrate on what is directly in front of me. Pick out a point just up ahead and aim to reach it. Just shut up and walk alongside him and don't be a laughing stock who embarrasses him in public ever again. "Girlies using you for laughing practice! Men use *them*, not the other way around." This on the day Bazza wins of all days. The day we win the mile at Randwick and then *this*. "Don't stagger," he growls, or else I can expect a hiding.

At the car I vomit. Vegetables, tomato skin, carrot and brown brine.

"Don't you dare do that in the car," he warns.

When emptied of vomit a chill of wellness enters me. I stand chilly and sweating. The Duke grabs my lapels and pulls me lower to get into the car. I push his hands away and tell him I can get in the car, this car or any car, by myself.

"Don't you push me," he says with narrowed eyes. He holds me by the lapels against the car door. I grab his lapels and pull at him, pull him off balance. He forces his forearm under my chin and heaves. My head is wrenched back. I push at his jaw with my palm and slip to the side to escape his hurting hold. He falls to one knee and roars "Jesus bloody Christ." His hat tips from him, drops upside-down on the gravel.

I kneel to help The Duke stand, saying "Sorry, sorry." But he repeats "Jesus bloody Christ" and crabs sideways to avoid kneeling in vomit.

He grips my lapels in his fists and shoves me, a punch-shove into my neck. I punch the top of his arm. He punch-shoves again. I punch his arm. Punch it again. He lets go of me and staggers to his feet, heaving. Such a stare to his eyes. Bloodshot anger. A hating stare. He shakes his head to rid the stare from his face. He wipes his open hand down his forehead, across his nose, cheeks, jaw. "Get in the car before we're thrown off the course." He picks up his hat. Spits it clean, pokes out the dents and curses, "It's stuffed."

I don't clip up my seatbelt because I want to put my hand on his shoulder. I want to embrace his shoulders and say sorry. I reach over and begin to say it but he unpicks my arm from where it has landed across his chest. "Come on," he says. "Enough of this. I said enough. Sit up. You want to play at being a man then play being a man who sits up and doesn't embarrass himself or me. Now, sit up." He pats my forearm. I am relieved to have that patting.

He starts the car. "I go in to bat for you at school and this is how you reward me on the day we won the mile. I'm referring to lunches in lockers. That's right. I took a call from your school. They were concerned about the episode. I promised them it's just a passing fad type of behaviour." He shakes his head, scoffing: "World in famine. Don't want to be wasteful." He points at me and places the end of his finger on my chest and taps it there in instruction. "You think about yourself. You think about *you*. You can't help famine people. And what are they ever going to do for you? Nothing. But you can help you. You should concentrate on *you*."

He puts the car in reverse and steers it on to the exit path. "You'll end up being seen as having peculiarities.

We all have peculiarities. Even your mother has peculiarities with her towels and funny moments. But we keep them to ourselves. We're a small family, son. Just the three of us. Remember that. Remember who you are. You're a man who shook the Prime Minister's hand today. Your mother will be thrilled to think we know him."

A FIRST YEAR, a pleb, stands before me chin out in an authoritative pose. His brassy-haired head is tilted back, his hands are in his pockets. His knee is bent forward and to the side. He is only a pleb, used by teaching staff to relay messages to boys, and yet he stands there like that as if superior to me. I am wanted by a master. I am to wait outside the staff room.

"Who exactly wants me?"

"I don't know exactly. A teacher whose name I don't know. You're to wait outside the staff room immediately."

I do not like that tone in his voice. Immediately. As if a pleb has the right to order *immediately* to me.

"Were you told to say immediately? Or was it just you adding it now? Your Chinese Whispers duty is designed to make you more servile to masters, not impertinent to me."

"It was them."

"It better be. Do you know the punishment for getting Chinese Whispers wrong?"

"No." That question has straightened his head and stiffened his knee.

"If the message is mis-told to the listener, you the Whisperer will receive the equivalent of a fine."

"What sort of fine?" His hands are out of his pockets.

"A detention on a Saturday. Or several detentions, or the cane."

He is standing up straight when he talks to me now. Another lie and that brass head will sink lower, as good as be bowed. "So when the master wanting the pleasure of my company says to me, 'What was the message you received? Word for word.' And I say 'Immediately' and immediately was not in the original message—get my drift?" There goes his head. Sinking, bowing, sunk.

"For good measure I might tell Sir that your message was so confused it sounded as if you said something about a bike beaten blue, irradiantly."

I have no idea what trouble I'm in, what punishment awaits me at the staff room. That is powerlessness worse than physical suffering for a sin. The fear of not knowing your fate. But powerlessness can be passed on down the chain. Passing down can halve the sense of it. Passing it down as I am now to this boy who is half my size. Better they piss their pants, the plebs, than enter the toilets and disturb a more senior boy who is smoking as I have been this lunchtime. Let alone render that senior boy powerless with a message. This ignorant pleb who has not yet learnt that he can be flicked with a lit butt. His face can be flushed in the bowl where paper is scrunched, paper with fresh brown wipings. I would tell him as much, say he was lucky his message was for a gentleman like me. I would take pity on him if he was not so stubborn. He is frightened. He is silent. His eyes are beginning to pop with pleading but he has not begged me "Please don't." He has not turned to me water-faced with weeping. The powerlessness has not been passed down the chain.

The twitch self is now in me. But I am not king of him yet. I am ashamed to want to be his king. And I am ashamed to have so far failed.

"Are you a boarder or a day boy?" I can read the answer on him. He is a Scrubber. He is a boarder. Nose and cheeks flecked with the sun's dots. Hands bigger than boy-hands, a bent bone in a finger, pale paddock scars. "Why did your parents send you away from home? For an education? What do farm boys like you want with an education! No, they sent you away because they didn't want you. They didn't love you. They, in effect, got rid of you. Out of sight, out of mind. You'll probably never hear from them again."

He glares at me, grimacing. In pain, or hatred of me?

My cigarette hisses in the bowl water. I flush and push away from the wall where I have been leaning.

Out of the toilets we go. Along the wide porch-path towards the corridors and stairs up to the staff room. The boarder is a step behind me.

"Perhaps they are splitting up and want you out of the way. Or having an affair. Who'd want you around, perving? Perhaps your father realised you're not really his son but the product of your mother fucking a shearer."

Finally they have arrived, tears. In blinked drops, too many to be kept wiped dry. A snot string dangles, is sniffed back into his nostrils. He folds his arms and hunches over slightly as if from cramp. He turns his back to me. To hide his shame of tears, or the better for hating me in more solitude, reject me in order to draw me closer and get his revenge by causing me guilt.

Not crying now but a howling. All because of a few words, this weeping so loudly in an uncontrollable, shuddering manner.

"Listen, I'm sorry for what I said. We all say bad things to each other. It's normal," I say trying to hush him. The strutters will gather around soon. They smell tears like a trail of blood. They will mock his cowardly nature, and my pitying him too.

I put my hand on his shoulder, lightly. "Shut up," I implore.

He tells me to fuck off and shrugs away my hand.

The strutters must be near, so many tears for them to smell on the wind.

There is no point in talking to him if he is going to behave this way. A no one, probably a shearer's son.

It is the drama teacher who wishes to see me.

I have never spoken to him before. Why would I?—he is a drama teacher? A bushy black arch of whiskers beneath his nose. Hair parted in the middle and let to grow below his earlobes more than The Mansions usually permits.

Here comes his hand. He wants me to welcome-dance as if we're to be friends, though he is a master. I have no choice but to link hands. "Good to meet you," he says. I do not respond. How could I? His hand is so weak, limp-weak, it hardly wraps mine around. "They say you've got a terrific voice for singing. If that's the case, I have a question."

I set my jaw, clenched and jutting for admonishment, for some trick where a compliment is turned on me.

"Would you consider singing in a play?"

I keep clenched. "Is that a new method of punishment?"

He throws his head back to laugh with closed eyes though I meant no joke. "The school is adapting *Catcher in the Rye* as a musical. You have been suggested as a possible Holden by the staff."

I am to take myself to the music hall and have Mr Birch listen if my register fits the music. "I presume you have read the book?"

"Oh yes. Of course."

"What did you think?"

I am a chosen one among all the others. I stroke my neck, the beautiful Adam's apple of its voice pipe so delicate but bony-hard. "What did I think about it? I thought it was a story of great truth."

Where are the strutters now? I want them to ask me: "Why are you so smiley?" Where is the Chinese Whisperer? I want to remind him that he doesn't say fuck off to me, someone mentioned by the masters to play a role in a play.

The book. I must read the book again, today. Now. This second. I want to believe its every word where I didn't believe any before. I vow I will. All beliefs begin by being forced.

★

Mr Birch sits at his piano as if fending it off, arms at full stretch, hands barely reaching the keys. His back is so straight his chin is pressed over his tie knot. His neck is too fat for his tie and spills over his collar as he rolls his fingers up the keyboard scale. In between rolls he pulls at his collar to relieve the red grab on his skin.

"Sing the scale to my playing," he commands. I take a breath and follow his fingers.

He stops playing before completing a roll and shakes his head. "No, no, no." He places his palms on his knees and sighs. "I'm sorry. But I was led to believe you could sing."

Led to believe? I give a jerk of my shoulders to punish him for his "Led to believe."

"I *can* sing," I say. I give another jerk, and a sneer-smile learnt from years of watching Feet. Perhaps he is testing me to assess my confidence and humour.

He tells me to sing again, all the way up the scale and down. But when I do, there is the same reaction from him. A "No, no, no" as if there is offensive wrongness in my every note.

"What have I done?" I jerk. I smile-sneer.

He turns up his palms, holds them out to indicate it is obvious what is wrong. "You sing from the throat."

It must gall music teachers to be only that, a teacher. A teacher at a school. Schools are all they are any good for. They bear a grudge for it which they take out on pupils. No opera house for them where they might instruct feted tenors in wigs and tights. Their lot is school boys, and some with more talent than they have ever had themselves. Mr Birch knows this of himself and resents it. He is one of *them*: he is a disappointed man.

"Elvis Presley sang from the throat. So did Nat King Cole," I remind him. Though there is no reasoning with a disappointed man. You must never give in to them. They're there to break the spirit in you. The spirit they lack. The mind, the heart.

"Yes, they did indeed sing from the throat," says Birch. He smirks. He is a disappointed man with a smirk. Far too satisfied a man given his position in life. "Indeed they did. But the difference in their case is, *they* could sing. Really, and greatly. Voices unique and pretty, if thin."

I lean across to grip an edge of the piano. Grip it to dig my fingernails into the wood until an ache reaches the quick.

This is a way to let the insult out, through the pain of crushing my nails into wood. Tears stay out of sight behind my eyes that way. My chin keeps from quivering. My twitch self jams in me before spit-breaths and cursing reach my lips. "I can sing as good as them," I say, a little juice of hatred filling my mouth. It takes two swallows to keep the spittle down.

Birch places his knuckles to his mouth to cover a mocking laugh.

I dig into the wood and sing the scale without his piano rolls, Elvis Presley-perfect. The vibrato droning with long delicate vowels.

Birch removes his knuckles. "This is a school play in Bellevue Hill, not the Mississippi."

I dig, waiting for him to say more, to admire at least the mimicking as remarkable. Does he want me to beg for praise? I will not beg. I would never beg to a disappointed man. Just a kind word or two is all I need. A complimentary phrase then the twitch self would ease.

He clasps his hands in his lap. "An impersonation very competent, I'm sure."

Is that praise? Yes, it is. I'm certain it is praising—*competent*. Yes it is. At last. "Thank you," I nod.

"But you should sing from down *here*," he says, hand on his chest as if making a promise. "Even from down here," hand on belly. He extends his arms in a swelling gesture. "You need to project yourself to a hall full of people. Not confine your talents to abominating hymns in chapel."

Talents. That is what he said: talents. It is definitely praise. I will present him with a "Yes, Sir" for that talents praise.

"To be an imitator is all very well but I want the original you. Do you have a *you*?"

A you? What is a you?

Birch makes a fist at his throat and speaks in a strangled voice. A person's *them*, their *you*, would never be situated in their throat. It would be situated in their chest. Their trunk. Their shoulders, stomach, bowels. "You have no *you*." He slaps his thigh. "Who are you?"

A question to shrug at, not answer. How is it answered except with shrugging?

This is what the *Catcher in the Rye* is about, Birch slaps. A boy who has no *him*, no *he*. Who has nothing going for him except that he is in a novel in search of how to become he. "You two are perfect for each other. So let us start that search now for your *you* voice."

He finger-rolls up the scale, grandly ending the performance with a ballet dancer's majestic curl of the wrist. He marches his fingers along the scale for my singing to follow. He beckons me with a nodding smile to keep up and stay in time.

I do keep up, but my voice is weak when singing this new way. A sound any boy might make, mounting the scale with a sweet, high-pitched vowel.

I must end this. I do not wish to sing in this play. Let the spittle rise up into my mouth. I will not stop it with fingernails in wood. Let me swear, teeth gritted, sucks of air bubbling through them.

But he keeps calming me with praising, this music teacher. Tricking me with his "Good. That's better. Keep going. There's the fellow."

He said of Holden Caulfield that he had nothing going for him. Applying it to me too with his "perfect for each other."

Tudor Park, is that nothing? A constituency I can be one of but above, is that nothing? Rain on a string? Prime Ministers of Australia if I want for friends?

Yet Birch's *goods* and *betters* bring up a boy sound from my belly. He tells me he is pleased, he sees progress in me. He presents a script to me and recommends that with holidays upon us I read it. He hopes I practise what I have learnt from him today: no throat; sing from down *here*. Next term we'll find the me in me if it's there.

THE LOOPHOLE ALSO works for clothes.

Feet's blue frock for evenings and her peach blouse with neck ruffles. Is there anything worse than having to wear the same piece of clothing over and over? She thinks not. Wearing it against one's ugly, wrinkly skin once, twice, on and on, rubbing in all one's odours just like towels. Replacing them is like keeping yourself new.

Of course, synthetics are dyed in deep and require a smidgeon of bleach to speed the balcony process. But girls behind the counter are none the wiser, and with the forcefulness of Feet's complaining she gets her way.

So important, new clothes, now the builders have finished the Tudor Park house to the point where it is livable. More a manor house than a plain word like house. What entertaining we're bound to do! People will be name-calling out the other side of their face. We'll be casting the net wider than cow people. "Believe you me, a house like we've built is one people travel to see. I can't wait to see them turn green," Feet says, clapping her hands together.

The thoroughbred yearling sales in Hamilton in January. Feet can only imagine who might drop in and stay. "There's bound to be Bart Cummings one minute. Tommy Smith and his crowd the next. Because now we're in a position where we're not to afraid to say 'Welcome to our humble abode.'"

The Duke stretches out in his chair and winks at her how glad he's going to be to have his good wife come out of her shell and enjoy the company of others once again. "My lady is back." He holds up his right hand, fits it into his left and shakes "Congratulations" to himself.

Feet unrolls the architect's plans on the dining-room table. She points to measurements on the scrolled paper, mouths them silently as if to keep them in her memory. She steps across the lounge in measuring strides, counts out 1, 2, 3. Turns right and steps, counts. Steps right again, counts. She mutters how wonderful it will be to have bathrooms you can swing a cat in.

She takes her box of crayons from the odds and ends drawer. Crayons for the special purpose of matching linen, cushion and rug colour to the walls, the ceiling, curtains, lampshades. She marks out strips of crayon colour on the plans to find the natural pairings. "I'll put ink-blue eiderdowns, blue rugs as well, against the oyster carpet," she says, tongue poked out in concentration. "My relations' mouths will water when they see it. I wonder where all my school friends have ended up. I'd love to see their faces."

She wonders if there is anything of The Duke's she can fade. It would be a shame not to have a few shirts, ones that really suit him, given her balcony treatment. One of his silk numbers perhaps. The purple paisley one she likes. She will get to work on it at once. We only have a week and we board the plane. She'll have to drop some bleach in. A shame the sun won't shine at night.

And on the subject of shame, why must her only son torment her? His face should be lit up. He should be running his fingers over the plans as excited as she is. He should be measuring out his bedroom. Stepping out the billiard room—a father and son's very own gentleman's nook. "How can you stand there sad as sacks? Makes me wonder why your father and I bother."

She tells me to please help her carry the clothes horse onto the balcony. And please show a bit of enthusiasm for the manor house. "You'll cut your mother and father to the quick."

I do have enthusiasm for the manor house, I say. I've proudly worn the scars from Tudor Park. I have displayed them like a love tattoo of the place.

The Duke has picked up his newspaper and flicked it to a page. He will stay behind that screen, reading and listening to me explain myself. He will scrunch the paper down into his lap if he needs to have a say.

Feet will attempt to embrace me when I tell her: "But I also have another enthusiasm. A singing enthusiasm."

I will have to let her do it, her wine-breath all over me. She will insist I thank her for inheriting her musicalness and when I don't thank her she will thank herself on my behalf. A manor house and a singer in one day! I brace for her outstretched arms, her smothering talcs and bittery scents.

"I want to learn to sing from down *here*," I announce, tapping my chest. "I need to see music shows, theatre plays, live plays, up close. I have been selected. That's right, *selected*."

The Duke bends one page-end down. I explain what it is I have been selected for.

Feet holds her end of the clothes horse mid-air to comprehend the news. She says to The Duke, "Special. Did you hear that?"

The Duke scrunches his paper into his lap. "Singing?" He frowns for more information.

"In the school play," I say. "I was selected."

Feet puts down the clothes horse. She stretches out her arms for me to be embraced. I bow my head and allow it to happen. She rubs my back for me to please return her hugging. I tell her I can't breathe with her pulling me so close. I put my arm around her and squeeze her until she gasps painfully, "Not so tight." That gets me free of her and the smothering smells.

The Duke laughs, "You can sing to the cows. They might milk more. I've heard cows like music in that way."

I scowl that I don't sing to cows. I'll be singing to a hall full of people. In Taonga there is a manor house. Here there are playhouses. This is a city not the sticks. There are singing teachers and theatres. I need to practise, to learn the singing craft or I will be laughed at and be remembered as a flop.

"Well, that's too bad," says The Duke. "You have to come to Taonga."

"Why?"

The Duke shakes his head and closes his eyes in a condescending manner. "As if I have to bother explaining that." He holds up a finger to count off a point. "Number one—you're sixteen and can't stay here by yourself."

"I could."

The Duke closes his eyes and says, "Ridiculous."

I dig my nails into the sides of my legs. My bottom teeth jut out in front of my top. "There'd be somewhere I could board."

Two fingers. "Number two. This is a very important occasion for us. The house we've set our hearts on. We're building up a showpiece for ourselves for years to come. We're doing this for you. Are you saying that is second fiddle to a bloody school play?"

Feet answers for me, "He is." She has begun her own digging, in her hair. She pants noisily out of her nostrils. "He's got tickets on himself. Forget everything we've done for him. Never mind Tudor Park. He's got tickets on himself."

The Dukes scrunches his paper to the floor. "See what you've done?" He closes his eyes and implores Feet, "Don't go all funny. There's no need to go funny."

She pants that she is not going funny and is not going to put up with insults that she's going funny. She simply feels gutted that her only son could not give a shitting damn about her beautiful manor house.

The Duke turns to me, "Tell your mother you give a damn."

That command has strengthened my digging, for I'm powerless under that command, the chain of command, the natural order. My twitch self is here. Yet there is no one to pass the powerlessness on to.

"Go and tell her you do give a damn. Do it now!"

I am silent, and intend to stay that way. Let it be a twitch silence that twists Feet's face into an angry face and brings on the dry weeping.

The Duke stands and puts his fists on his hips. "Look, you've got 300 acres to sing to your heart's content. And you've got your mother to sing to, to give her a lovely song."

No, no, no, I dig. "I don't want to sing like that anymore, from the throat."

Feet's face twists tighter, but I am not trying to twitch her now. I want to explain about the *me* kind of singing as opposed to the other kind.

The Duke points and jabs that that kind of talk—the not wanting to sing to your own mother talk—is hurtful and nonsense. "Stop all this having tickets on yourself business. Singing to your mother is what you've been given the gift for. Not for having tickets on yourself. Not for putting a play before your own mother, before family and Tudor Park."

I dig and sneer that one minute they want me away from Taonga and its gold-diggers. And the next thing I'm being made to go there.

Feet scratches the static in her scalp. "He'd bloody well sing for that little slut who wrote him letters. She'll put her claws into him with her 'Such a wonderful voice you have' and 'I hope to hear it again soon.' Sing for a little peasant bitch, but not for me."

"What letters? I never got letters."

Feet throws back her head triumphantly. "You certainly did not, I saw to that. Some little bitch, Bettina." She shivers and pulls a face as if the very act of naming her brings a bitter chill. "I dealt with her. Those letters found their way straight to where they belonged—the bin. I thought we'd had our talks about urges and gold-digger peasants. I thought we were safe. But obviously not. To hell with it all then. We *should* stay in Sydney. Not some shit bastard place with bitches who write love letters on paper with cheap shitting perfume sprayed on."

I step left, then two steps right. My nails so deep in my thighs my finger bones ache. I bite down hard, teeth into teeth, an electric shock jolts me from a filling. "Fuck," I yell. "Fuck, fuck. They were my letters."

Feet screams "Language!" and presses her hands to her ears. "How dare he say language in my presence. Language in front of me."

The Duke leaps over the coffee table, fists clenched, a fury-face. "Take that language back or so help me!"

Feet pants and spits, "Language. The bastard uses language in front of me." She sweeps up the manor house plans from the table and crushes them against herself. She rips them, flings a handful to the floor.

The Duke heel-spins from me to hurry to her. He grabs her ripping hands and prises out shreds of plans, rescues paper balls of them and pushes them into his pockets. He demands she "Stop this" but his bellowing only makes her scream for me to get my bastard, filthy mouth out of her hearing. "Shitting bastard using language in front of me."

IF BLOOD IS red, why are veins blue?

Water is clear but the grass it falls to green. Feet and The Duke—how is it they made me? A natural order exists that turns such ordinary people into my new breed.

Nor is silence a way of finding a way out of silence. It is a language all its own. The language of *distance* between The Duke and Feet and me. If I must speak, I would demand they provide me with what money I need. Clothes, food, and submit to the new breed that supersedes them in me.

However, if I am to find the me voice, I must not let sound die in me from unuse in silence. Die even before it is born.

They have won. Those two ordinaries. I am here on this farm. I must give up my determined silence. I put it in place because the twitch self insisted I punish them.

This blank mask of resentment, I cannot keep it up. It is the blank mask of a fraud. For the manor house thrills me too much. Its front door like the vast slab entrance of churches. Staircase rising eighteen steps to a little landing.

It bends there for seven steps more. On the left my bedroom, vast enough for a dozen Queen beds. Bathroom with gold taps called Pharaoh's Fingers. Main bedroom beside it with a wall made of window. Window too at the end of a wardrobe you walk through. The patchwork of paddocks spreads below. Window in the ceiling to let in the sky. The ceiling sprayed in a gravel-paint known as frosting.

Downstairs beyond the gallery, two guest rooms we'll call the South Wing. The nook for billiards—red walls with redder velvet flower patterns to set off the table's green baize. A long, low light with tassels just like professionals. A step up to a viewing area. Cane furniture where Feet can watch over games.

The Tudor façade outside with its skinny strips of timber, brown crossed over white. Tin roof fringed with shaggy wood for an effect of faux thatching.

The twitch self orders me to be silent when Feet asks, "What do you think of your room?" It demands I confine my answer to a shrug, an "It's OK" at the most, and look down, not around me, admiringly. This I do.

The Duke says, "Is that all you can say?" He shakes his head exasperated that he cannot *reach* me. I do not wish him wounded or soul-sick whether he's an ordinary or not. But the twitch tells me I should wish it. It says, "Ignore his hurt and soul-sickness."

Feet is looking to the heavens and wondering where did she go wrong to deserve such an ingrate for a son. The second self is coming for her. She greets it with her bared teeth, her usual claw of fingers.

I do something the twitch self mocks as weak. I feel a poisoning in my stomach which the twitch self dismisses as nothing but guilt. Guilt is a bug not potent enough to make me throw up, but one that sends up waves of mild nausea.

After what Feet did to my letters, guilt is the last bug I should let into my system. Hated is more like it. The twitch agrees. Yet, just as the ghost train is ready to rush her away, I tell her the bedroom is beautiful. Such a view—the great grin of the mountains. I am its audience of one. I feel I should offer it applause. The ghost train leaves without her.

I pass the guilt down to Bettina. If only that peasant gold-digger knew the trouble she had caused. Sending me letters, causing a rift between a mother and her son.

But when Feet asks me if I think her plastic flower arrangement is lovely, and her new flower-stands—Roman columns made of metal that appear to be of stone—I answer No. No too to the fabric hydrangeas that never die or shed a leaf, that need no water, just washing.

I want Feet arrested for stealing my letters. A thief mother. I dig my nails beneath my shirt to go deep into skin. I re-instate the silence.

But then the guilt recurs. Police? A thief? Look at the woman's pleasure, I demand of the twitch self. "Look at it." So simple a pleasure in humble plastic flowers.

"Did you say something?" asks Feet.

"Yes. Those columns are quite nice."

She bought a novelty lamp in Sydney. An ancient naked Greek figure standing in a cage with bars of light. "That's nice as well," I say.

But an hour later, seething silence because I think of her reading Bettina's pages. Pages that might have had crosses for kisses on them, hand-drawn sunshine and hearts. I seethe through dinner. I eat in small mouthfuls as if the food is not to my taste.

By now Feet is exhausted, confused. To be on the verge of many ghost journeys all day and every journey cancelled by me just in time—I have the timing down perfect.

"Will you sing to me?" she asks, wearily, flopping on the new blue three-seater to doze. "Singing would block out that dreadful whoosh-whoosh sound of the washing machine."

I certainly will not sing for her. Robber and reader of letters. Singing for the sake of clothes washing.

Let her swoon all she likes at the thought of a serenading. Sung to sleep as if drugged by me, a snake charmer for humans. I will not sing for her.

I sing *Love Me Tender*.

I sing *Embraceable You*.

I AM NOT asking for the plum job at Tudor Park. I have no desire to drive those deformed humans to milking for instance. Let Norman have it. Let William if he wishes, nudging and prodding them forward like a chain gang without chains.

Nor do I want the bottom rung—hosing muck from the shed yard after milking is done. The grass gone to liquid, green custard curdled in stinking bowels. An hour it takes. The hose water so icy my fingers swell and itch with chilblains as if the skin will any second split.

Poached Eye and Sensible have been sent away to trainers with reputation. Churchill gets his five dollars now to paint our post and railings for half a morning. No need for me to oversee him. Let him hate-talk timber. He can curse and kick the woodness all he likes. Fences feel no rancour. They have pine for ribs and eyeless knots for eyes.

No, the job I covet is feeding the new-weaned calves. The females kept to feed up into milkers. The males, called Bobbys, are reared a few days and no more. They are crowded into a tray on the tractor for driving to the roadside. There a truck collects them to be veal meat. The driver checks that the birth cord dangling from under their fur has wizened healthily like a stick of pizzle. He weighs them for the abattoir's over-58 pounds rule.

When feeding the calves I can sing.

I bolt a vat on wheels to the Massey Ferguson tractor. It has a boom of fat rubber nipples. I pour milk into the vat, add buckets of water to string the milk out, a lukewarm sick-smelling brew.

I drive this sloshing load up the race to where calves are gathered at their paddock gate. Hooves sunk in the mud of their waiting. A steam rising from their mooing moans. Their eyes rolled back with the effort of the noise.

Especially Miss Beautiful. Her eyes go white and shut to moan the loudest. Miss Beautiful. I have named her so for her tawny coat, white socks and matching face-blaze. Taller than a normal Jersey, she shoves her way to the front to greet me and sing her one long note. I mimic the note in reply. Again. Again. As if common meaning has suddenly crossed between species.

I unlatch the gate. It swings out, grates across the race's stones. The calves dash forward to suck the vat's edges, tyre nuts, the boom's nippled elbow, my gumboot toes. I have to shoo them with a wild yell, slap them on the nose. I hold the note of the yell by tensing my stomach. I think it is a *C* I'm making, which when I squeeze out the last of my breath, peters out and becomes a lower note, a *B*, a *B-flat*.

I wade through the calf-wave singing, counting to check there are thirty creatures—counting the numbers in song. I have to protect my groin from their butting mouths. I fend off Miss Beautiful—she sucks my fingers, the ends of my jacket, my walking knee though only dry comes out. Once the boom is lowered she scurries in the scrum of them all towards a free teat where milk sprays and tongues poke to the side and foam as they suck.

There are fewer nipples than mouths so I must distract loose suckers until a feeding calf is full. The sign for full is when the bloat of enough drinking puffs out the triangle-dent in front of their hips. Too much bloating and it dies. I let the calves suck my fingers, two fingers at a time—fore-finger and middle for one calf, little finger and its neighbour for another. Twisting the fingers deep past their lipless pout and into their mouths to feel the hot serrated gums, sandy tongue and hard seam where no teeth have formed. The pads of my fingers wrinkle from the wet pull. Heat seeps into me from the frenzied feeders who are certain I have milk on my insides.

That heat and that pull! I bend my groin away from it, out of reach of the suckers because when they push close and touch me with their dripping noses and tongues I can imagine it is a real human doing it, making my penis tingle and swell until it is no longer a penis but a cock. *Cock* because the senses want a rougher language for lust than penis, a mere medical name.

Squeezing my eyes shut doesn't help.

It takes more than squeezed eyes to stop wanting the cock out of its trousers and let a calf have its way onto the new finger. Not any calf, but Miss Beautiful, a calf above calves. Not of the cows but an evolved kind, a superior breed. "Someone could be watching," I say to her, kneeing to keep her at a distance.

I busy myself with pushing a bloated calf from its position on the boom for the next in line.

Miss Beautiful, we are far enough from the milking shed for no one to see us. But don't magpies have sight? There are gaps in the hedgerows. An ancestor, dead and floating invisibly, might be above us this instant, checking me, his kin, to be heartened that he is watching the admirable progress of his loins.

I force the *me* voice to bellow out of my chest and stomach. I force and force. I sing the scales three times. Then mixed notes, randomly from the scale, till the cock has gone back to penis, and the ancestor can leave proud enough with what he has seen.

Clover's tiny green fan normally has three leaves.

Three leaves like three servings of itself. Four leaves sometimes though it's rare and therefore means good luck for the humans who pluck one like a soft coin given up to them from the wishing-well soil.

There she is at it again—Feet parting the pasture with her fingers. She kneels stiffly, pushing her palm down on one knee for balance. Four leaves bring great fortune or little blessings, she believes. Good health, much money which is what a life is for.

She keeps them, her treasure, between the pages of her books: the only books she owns—those Nana recipes with cellotape binding.

"Come and help me look," she asks of me. "Don't you want your mother to be happy, healthy and rich? Come and pick clover with me so I won't be left alone."

But I am already gone, hurdling a fence, hand on post to spring, scissoring my legs. Gone to feed the calves, to sing and finger their mouths and let them nibble my groin in their huddle of hunger. Miss Beautiful again the most insistent of lovers, until my ancestors-thinking saves me.

Feet is beginning to wonder about four-leaf clovers. We have hardly been inundated with curious guests: "What's the point of building a lovely manor home if there's no one to come and say Wow!? It's like we add up to nothing for all our efforts in life. That's the very way I feel sometimes."

She and The Duke base their arguments on it, whether it's awfulness in people that makes them stay away in droves. Feet complains that it is, and that when you're stuck in North Island, New Zealand you are really much too far away for guests who are anyone worthwhile—"We might as well be at the South Pole."

The Duke makes two points and leaves the arguing at that. One: people just don't arrive, you have to invite them. We're not royalty. People don't ask for an audience. "You've been too long going into yourself. *You* need to go to the world. It doesn't come to you." Two: no one's ever good enough for her. It's an off-putting trait. "If you act like you're royalty, people turn up their nose."

"That's ridiculous," Feet stomps. "I'm the least off-putting person I know. I expected more happiness at this stage in my life and I'm beginning to resent it not coming."

She now refers to clover as "those bastard things, those frauds" but she still parts pasture unless it's raining.

Today she has only picked for half an hour and there is a sound. She lifts her head and listens to the air. A ripping sound of car tyres between paddocks on the milk-shed drive. The vet's car, a grey station wagon with mud doors from the morning's potholes.

Five four-leaf clovers so far this session and it has delivered someone—a vet visitor. Better than nothing. An educated man, a professional. Thick spectacles and a nodding, smileless manner of speaking to emphasise the confidence of his pronouncements.

He may wear overalls, but they lend him a green surgical appearance—he is no tradesman. He is a science man. So many pens poking from his chest pocket. When he removes his overalls before getting in his car, his slacks and shirt beneath are spotless. His radio plays classical music.

Feet hurries to the kitchen to set out cups and boil the kettle. She will butter a scone batch kept in the freezer for such occasions.

The Duke has not been well today. He is having a lie-down, but she'll rouse him for welcoming the vet into our house. We can't have someone sleeping and snoring when there's a guest to show around.

★

Today five cows with marks for medicine sprayed on them. Two mastitis; two pessaries for afterbirth still hanging from

CRAIG SHERBORNE

backsides after calving. A milk fever Jersey who gets the staggers and falls down.

The fallings down are getting longer between the standings, says Norman. His cigarette sore is missing from his lip. He knows a worker should never address a professional man, a vet man, with that ugly sight stuck to his face. A worker needs to answer Yes or No clearly to professional questions and not be disrespectful with the pause it takes to draw smoke and sigh it, to speak with a cloudy mouth. "Doc," is how Norman ends his answers. "She's getting weaker by the hour, Doc."

Doc nods that that is obvious just by looking at her sitting with her legs tucked under in the mud of the culling yard.

"Chewing her cud like she's taking some sun, but on death's door if you ask me," Norman says with a gruntlaugh. "That's the way of things. They're a dumb animal."

Doc agrees that what he says is true—she might indeed not be long for this world. This gives Norman cause to stand up straight in a moment of pride that a vet is not the only one who knows a thing or two. He turns to smile this to his Bill who grins acknowledgment. He turns to smile it to me but I ignore him.

I'm holding my breath till my face hurts from too much blood in it. Norman probably thinks I am red with embarrassment that I lack his farm learning, but I'm in training.

I have decided to build up my lungs for singing. I have just walked a full minute down the drive to the milk shed without taking a single breath.

Norman must consider himself the equal of a vet. Just because of one moment of pride he is now equal to Doc and can take charge and grab the cow's penis-tail and lift to try and urge it to all fours.

Doc waves him to stop: "It's not a lever that tail. You're not helping her one bit."

Norman keeps hold of the tail though stops yanking it erect. His mouth is a hole in his beard as if he's about to speak. Only a wheeze and grumble come out. He does let go of the tail but only because Doc is staring at him, waiting for his instructions to be carried through. The tail snaps shut over the cow's backend.

Doc walks to his station wagon and its cupboards and drawers of drug vials, syringes, kidney dishes, sponges.

Norman takes a sore from his tin, one brown from previous puffings. He leans close to his Bill. "Cunt thinks he knows everything," he says quietly, striking a match and drawing up light through the lamp of his cupped hand. Bill nods that cunt's the right word, and shapes to give a quick kick into the cow's side in time with a repeat of the swearing but Doc is about to return. He carries two bottles of calcium tonic to the cow and sets them down beside her neck. He takes a rubber tube from his overalls' pocket and a long, thick needle.

He twists the cow's neck using the backs of his knees to push. He sights the artery groove in the neck skin and throws the needle dart-like. He manoeuvres the dart up, down, sideways, until dark blood dribbles out. He connects the needle to the tube and ask-orders Norman to stand close with the bottle, open the bottle and fit the flanged end of the tube to it. He's to hold it high and let the tonic gurgle until empty.

Norman does so but not before licking the sore to a fresh sucking spot and working it into a cloud billowy enough for inhaling and blowing in Doc's direction. He tells Doc the tonic won't do any good. In his experience a cow down for this long is fit only for the dead cow lorry.

"You could be right," Doc says.

Norman winks and nods to Bill: some sentence is exchanged between them that needs no speech to be clear to them, a "Doc might not be a dill after all" or "Vets have the learning but *I* have the years."

Doc fingers the cow's eyelids wide open and diagnoses that she's bright enough in herself.

Norman agrees, she is. "But she don't stand on her eyes." He winks again at Bill who covers his mouth against letting laughter out.

Doc concedes that the dead lorry might be all she's good for if he thinks she's going to suffer.

"Too true," Norman says, and nods his allegiance with Doc against her suffering.

But men's allegiances can last only seconds. Men fall out with each other. They get back on side. They fall out. Go back to firm as friends. Doc taps the cow's eye corner to test that the eye blinks alertly. "You know," he says. "I'd be giving her one more go." He ask-orders Norman to go and get the hip clamps.

"Hip clamps?" Norman hoiks and spits a small cough to the ground. He makes an f-sound but doesn't say the full *fuck*. Bill copies the mouthing and turns in time with Norman to have his back to Doc. He too hoiks and spits. He stands knuckles on hips.

Norman spits that the cow is too far gone for hip clamps. "Might as well fetch the rifle now."

Doc says there is no sense in putting a good animal to the rifle, not before giving her the benefit of the doubt.

Norman licks his sore in disagreement and wonders for the life of him why a so-called educated man like Doc, a professional fellow, would bother with a poor beast that was good as dead. A man can read books about an animal but books can't teach you what working hands-on with them every day will.

Doc repeats: hip clamps.

Norman licks that he supposes vets have got to earn a living. He makes a jerking movement with his head for William to fetch the hip clamps from the implement shed. "If the poor bitch is going to be made to suffer, so be it." He holds out his arms and lets them slap down against his sides.

Doc pats the cow's forelock and says she's not suffering very much for now.

My allegiance is with Doc over a Norman. A learned man over a toucher of teats who has given up so easily on a bright-eyed cow. Who owns the cow in the first place? The Duke. And therefore me. This toucher is in no position of power to decide life or death over property of Tudor Park. I have a responsibility to remind him of that. "Where I come from we don't give up that easily," I say, a little out of breath from my breath-holding practice.

"It's your people's money. Waste it how you like." Norman hoiks again. "Let it suffer."

Doc would be impressed by some philosophical display from me here. "Wouldn't suffering be better than death?"

Norman grunts, "How would you like to spend your life just lying there?"

Of course I wouldn't like it, and I'm not a medical man, but I remind him that plenty of people live lying down in an iron lung. Plenty of people live propped up in wheel-chairs.

Doc agrees that what I say is true. He speaks with that smileless authority that I can see makes Norman furious. So furious he spits out his wet sore and attaches to his lip a new one from his tin and gets involved in the distraction of lighting it.

We are truly aligned, Doc and I. Two educated men against this toucher of teats, this disappointed man. Doc walks to his car. I follow. He places his needle and tube in the boot. Vials of white fluid rattle in their compartments.

"Is that penicillin?" I ask, because Doc will be pleased to know I have knowledge of scientific history, the history of penicillin. From Fleming to Florey. I have read about the miracle that turned mould on a cheese lunch into the white in those vials. Jesus turned water into wine, but penicillin was more useful. I've heard people, stupid people confuse Pasteur as the discoverer. "How can you confuse Pasteur with the mould?" I shake my head for more allegiance from Doc. "Penicillin is not Pasteurisation. Some people! What a joke."

Doc says "Indeed," as if he has no interest in discussing the issue further. Who else in this district would know his Fleming from his Florey; his Pasteur from his penicillin? Knowledge enough surely for a vet to take an interest in the knower. I accept he must be a busy man, always pressed for time, his services prized. But he is not talking to a Norman or a Bill now. This vet, this science man, is talking to me.

*

Feet will be expecting him for refreshments. We have a new manor house—a person of Doc's standing would be expected to want to tour it. Do so as a man would tour a place of significance, an impressive location, an architectural site. A man who listens to classical music is a connoisseur of the finer things. Surely he won't be hurrying away. Surely he will do us the courtesy of at least a cup of tea, postpone his next appointment in favour of Tudor Park hospitality.

"You're not rushing? There are refreshments waiting for you up at the new house." I use a frown that I hold in place until he stops his fidgeting among rattling vials and rackety drawers. I hold it until he stands up straight and concentrates on me.

"I've work to do," he says.

"Well, there's more to do here," I say. There isn't more work to do, but I will invent work if I have to, just to make him apologise for hurrying if nothing else. He may want to rush on to appointments, but he is refusing our family's food and drink. He is not going to leave at *his* convenience. He'll leave at ours, mine. Such punishment might make him more social to us next time.

"A sickly calf," I say. In the hut there is a sickly calf he might cast an eye over. A sickly calf by other people's terms perhaps, but not so much by mine. From birth the calf has been unable to suckle. Being a *he* he was doomed for the bobby calf truck but is already a week old and way off making the proper weight. Sickliness has therefore been his saviour. And I intend to be his saviour from now on. I'll transform him with my tending. Twice a day I feed him like a baby, squeezing his weak mouth to grip and suck a bottle. I tell Doc this in a low voice not for Norman's hearing. Calf feeding is my job and not Norman's. I'll spare myself his mocking that I'm wasting time and effort on a runt. The low voice is also in keeping with the reverence I have for the task. I am the calf's only chance. I am the nurturer. No one cares for him but me. I am his Jesus of Taonga. I will save him and I will keep him. He will survive and be so grateful he will become a follower of me. I will give him a proper name to go by because to go by "calf" or "sick calf" demeans.

"He's in the hut over here," I say. Holding my hand out as if inviting him into my privacy.

The hut is a tiny tin place: you must duck your head to be under its roof. The floor is a row of slats with narrow gaps between them so piss can flow through or be hosed away with the scours of splattery yellow and scours more blood than digested food.

The sick calf lies on his side, his shaggy brown coat sunken around his bones. He should be gambolling his freedom from the bobby truck, instead he hardly lifts his head. He has doom-eyes, a dark acceptance of his fate, set well back in their sockets as if to protect them.

I lift him so he can balance on his pale, floppy pincers. He stands shakily, my fingers hooked around his ribs.

Doc has covered his nose and mouth with his hand. He lets out a muffled gagging. "Putrid," he muffles. "Worst I've smelt in some time."

I close the wood door to keep Norman from prying, he and his defeatist attitudes. But Doc bunts the door open with his shoulder.

"Let the air get out through here for Christ's sake," he gags. "Don't you have a sense of smell?"

"I can't smell a thing," I reply. Of course I can smell. The stink would sicken anyone. But I have not brought him in here to criticise my sense of smell.

"The calf is rancid," Doc gags.

"He can't help it," I say as a reprimand, cupping the calf's chest in one hand and petting his bony head with the other. Petting not too hard or else the force makes the head drop.

Doc stares at me. He speaks through a handkerchief. "*He* can't help it. But *you* certainly can. You can help him by knocking the poor beggar on the head. This minute. This is no way to treat an animal, cooped up in filth, starving to death."

I give this vet an angry stare of my own. "I'd never hurt an animal."

"This calf is dying and suffering in the process."

"It's getting better. Yesterday he couldn't stand at all."

"He's not standing now, it's just you're holding him."

I want this man out of my hut, away from my calf. Interfering with how I do things. Telling me to kill the very thing I want to make well. I tell him not to bother with this patient. *I* will look after him. "I'm sorry I troubled you with it." Then I clench my teeth, bow my head and go on petting the head-bones for the vet to become fed up and leave.

But he doesn't leave. He coughs into his handkerchief and steps aside for Norman to get good footing on the slippery slats and come closer for a look.

Norman waves his hands in front of his nostrils. "You'll have the protection of animals mob on to you at this rate, boy."

He says that "boy" like a signal to me that he and Doc are back aligned. The two of them aligned against me. I stay clenched and bowed.

Doc orders me to let go of the calf and let it drop. I refuse. He orders again. "Let it go." I clench. Doc orders more loudly this time that I'm to let the bloody creature go.

"It will flop down," I clench. A mistake to say that. I knew the instant I said it.

Doc takes the handkerchief from his face and holds out his arms. "Exactly. It will flop down. It's at death's door. The kindest thing is to kill it."

I let the calf go. It flops, its legs tangled in its legs. Tongue lolling. Its mouth slowly closing, head sinking to rest on its side.

Doc says accusingly, "It should never have got this far."

"Amen," nods Norman. "Too busy off with the fairies singing, this boy." He shimmies his fingers across the air. "Hear him all over the farm, singing, singing."

That my *me* sounds have reached his ears, have drifted inside his hearing, inside anyone's hearing except the calves

I sang among, violates me, like leering into my private soul.

"I don't know what on earth you're talking about," I laugh. "You must have voices in your head if you think I'd be wasting my time singing when there's work to do. I have a responsibility to master every element of Tudor Park's business."

Norman sniggers through his beard hole the words *Tudor Park*, and shimmies his fingers again as if the name is too fanciful for his listening.

Doc raises his voice that singing or no singing, someone has to deal with this miserable calf. He himself is happy to do the deed, though he shouldn't have to explain the economics involved in giving lethal injections every time a sick calf needs to meet its maker.

"Here, here," Norman says.

Doc tells me to fetch a rifle if I have one and give this calf some relief. Or else he'll feel obliged to have a word to my father about the rights and wrongs of keeping suffering animals hanging on.

The Duke told I caused an animal of his, of ours, to suffer? Me reduced to Churchill in his eyes?

"No, no," I smile to Doc. "It'll be done immediately. My old man isn't feeling too well today. Please don't disturb his sleeping." I assure him he has made himself very clear on the calf issue. Given The Duke is not well, there would be no point calling in for a cup of tea after all. Best he hurry

on to his next patient. Doc nods that he's taking me at my
word. He gets in his car and is gone.

Bill has fitted hip clamps to the front-end loader. He
has lowered the loader arms and screwed the clamps to the
cow's hips and lifted her. Her hind legs paw weakly at the
ground to grip it. Her front legs fare better—they walk but
walk harnessed to the one spot.

Norman goes to the tractor and takes from its tool-box
a hammer like a skinny dog's head. With this in his fist he
comes back to the hut, gumboots clapping against his shins
from his long strides.

He opens the hut door and ducks through it sucking on
his unsmoking sore. He crouches in the doorway, his eyes
crossed to peer down for any sight of a glowing on his lip.
"You're not cut out for this way of life," he says. "You've
got no stomach for it. You don't belong here with your *Tudor
Park* nonsense and singing. Animals aren't pets. A calf's a
fucking calf. It's a nothing. You put it out of its misery—
whack on the noggin—and that's the end of the matter."

He has passed the shame down to me. It is he, not me,
who holds the hammer but it's me who feels shame. Shame
that I have no stomach, no farmer's courage for killing. An
old, disappointed man like Norman is going to do my deaths
for me.

There must be no great feeling to it, killing. Just a ritual
inherited from the tribes of the ages. Even learned men—
politicians, judges, Caesars, show little mercy bringing death

to the condemned. Here I am baulking at a bag of stunted calf bones.

"Wait. Let me. I'll do it." I ask to be handed the hammer.

Norman holds the hammer out of my reach. He speaks quietly, almost gently that there's no need for me to prove myself on the issue. He's lost count of how many calf heads he's cracked in his life. This will be just another.

I insist. Not with words but a determined tilt of my head to show I've set my mind on it.

"Good on you," Norman says, shuffling sideways to let me crouch through the door. We have an allegiance now. I take the hammer in my fist, a heavier object than I remember hammers ever being.

I summon the pull of history to raise my arm. I am raising my weapon to club life out for the first time. My initiation killing. I am history. There is history after all in this place. I am human. I am ancient.

The blow-thud stamps a white circle between the calf's eyes like a raw target. But one blow only starts the killing. It does not finish it. The calf's eyes roll back. Breath pops and bubbles from the dying nose, but another blow, and quickly another blow is needed to make sure. Three off-centre rounds dent the skin, white on white. There is no blood. Small hairs stick to the hammer's sheen.

Norman drags the kill outside by the leg. Too small to bother with the dead cow lorry—we'll have to dig a hole.

He compliments me on my strong right arm. It usually takes him four or five goes.

I breathe so fast I could believe the calf's breathing has passed up to me and now I have extra.

Does doc have a way to diagnose humans, so close are we to the animals? Could he tell the difference in me now— that I am a human with extra breathing? Breaths that heave in and out of me with each remembering of the hammer head coming down. In my ears the gushing noise of my heartbeats. Can a stethoscope sense if it is fear or shame, exhilaration?

Next time he calls to cure Tudor Park cows I have questions to ask this educated man: does he get extra breathing when he puts cows, dogs, horses, down? Does killing steal more life up into us from the corpse and make us stronger? Or is the extra breathing the victim's last gasp slipped inside us to poison our memory?

And does nature try to balance the scales? Can it pass on the sickness of the killed thing to our loved ones? The Duke was unwell before but now he is worsening. He lies in an S to smother the pains in him with his knees. He vomits, then his face pinkens back to normal. Then he points to his chest. Then to a fire in what Feet calls his downstairs department. With the pain his eyes become blurred, he says. "It's like looking under water." He is cold but he sweats.

He does not want an ambulance. Feet is not to disobey him. I am not to disobey him. If his heart is giving out, he'll be damned if he spends his days as an invalid who can't even mount stairs. If it's cancer, let it end here and now. Not some drawn-out miserable business.

His eyes half close in sleepy, weakening blinks. He mumbles to himself that if he is to die, let it be in his Tudor Park bed. Let it be on his land, his piece of Earth's earth. Bury him in a paddock where the water below makes that wonderful trickle. He has made something himself, of his life. He can die a happy man.

Feet starts her left and right stepping. But no matter how much she scratches in her hair, no matter how much she tells him she is holding back a torrent of tears, The Duke mumbles that he couldn't be happier to have it end right now with the two people he loves at his side.

But we are not at his side. Feet steps and scratches at the foot of the bed. I step and scratch too, dig my nails into my scalp. The Duke curls a finger for us to come closer and sit with him and be a family together. He wants Feet and I to fit into the top space of his S. "How can I sit and listen to you talk this way?" Feet stomps. "Such a cruel way to talk when I'm worried sick and you're carrying on as if you haven't a care in the world. You're in seventh heaven while I'm sick with worry."

The Duke has no interest in listening. He curls his finger for me to come closer. He wants me to know that he couldn't be prouder to think he will leave this world with me in charge of what he has built up. Me, his flesh and blood, who is so young but a leader of men.

Feet chokes into weeping, real weeping with streaming tears. She yanks her hairdo free of its swirlings and sobs how she hates life, hates it. Life that's condemning her to be alone, to raise a child alone. She has done all the right things—she has worked and saved, worked and saved, and now life has turned viciously on her and her shit bastard dreams.

The Duke says he expects me to look after my mother as *he* would care for her and make up in her heart for losing her husband.

Feet yanks her hair and asks God for everything to be in order. "Everything is in order, isn't it?" she asks The Duke, but he is groggily chanting "Couldn't be prouder, couldn't be prouder." Feet yanks that she has not paid attention to affairs as she used to. She has not been herself and has left things to The Duke. Surely all is in order with his will. Such a basic thing. Surely that is the least of her concerns. But where is a copy held? She steps left and right and curses this shit bastard day as the worst in her shitting life.

The Duke grimaces into a tighter S.

Feet scuffs in frantic static out of the bedroom and onto the stairs' landing. She yells that she is too frightened and confused now to care what The Duke has demanded she do or doesn't do. She weeps that she is going to call an ambulance whether he likes it or not. If she could only remember where the phone is. Where is the phone in this bastard shit of a house! You can never find a bastard phone in a new house! And what do you dial? "I can't think! I can't shitting bloody think!"

I sob such fat tears they land with a plop on The Duke's sheets. I hold his hand. Chilled sweat has greased his fore-arms and flattened down their black hairs. I shake him to wake him up and tell him to vomit into the bucket by the bed and feel well again. I tap him with the back of my hand as if a joke might rouse him: "If you don't get better, I really will think you've got no gumption."

The phone's bells ding and ding downstairs—Feet bang-ing the receiver down to punish its not knowing what to do without her.

✶

THE AMBULANCE DRIVER straps The Duke into a trolley though he pleads to be left in his bed. Pleads that he be let stay curled in his soothing S and not straightened into a painful shape. The driver injects him into acceptance.

Feet pulls me close to her in time with saying that we must pull ourselves together, her and me. She lays her arm across my shoulders. She smells of fresh coatings of face powder and sprayings of perfume. Her eyes are newly ringed in brown from her bathroom pencils. Her hair bun is re-wound and stacked and sprayed erect. Chains snibbed to her wrists. Jewels clipped to her ears. She says we must pull ourselves together whatever the bastard of a future brings. We must not cry in public where people will see us and snigger that you can have all the money in the world but unless you've got your health. "The operator on the phone—she could tell I was rattled. She's at the local exchange so you can bet the world she's already spread the word: fancy pants's husband is in trouble and she's gone a bit funny."

We will travel to hospital in the ambulance with The Duke.

Turning out of our driveway onto the road Feet notices the ambulance has dark windows and so if anyone's got their binoculars out they'll be sorely disappointed. She pokes her fingertips into her forehead. Red fingerprints smudge through the powder. She pokes her forehead and talks under her breath.

"Are you praying?" I sniffle.

She purses her lips and says, yes, she is. "The first and last time I will do it, I don't mind telling you, because I don't think it's fair. I don't know what I have done to deserve this. And I'll be stuffed if I'm going to bloody well pray again if this is the way any shitting bastard of a God treats us."

She takes her compact from her handbag and re-dabs her forehead. A square of lace handkerchief is tucked under her watchband. She flicks it free of its folds and blots The Duke's greasy brow. She winces and shakes her head wishing she had not said what she just said about God, just in case there is a God. It will bring bad luck on us. It's asking for trouble. She wishes she had brought her four-leaf clovers with her to make up for it. She may have a spare one in her bag. She searches, but no.

The Duke's eyes are half shut as if drunk in restless sleep. I whisper in his ear in my own kind of praying, my eyes squeezed closed as if to squeeze out thoughts from my brain into the atmosphere for transmission. "You can't leave," I say. "I am not ready for Tudor Park. I'm out of place here."

I confess to him that his very sickness could well be my doing because of the calf killing. Just as strange things happen in Taonga such as water trickling out of sight when you tread the ground, there may well be a system of animal justice dealt to humans. Not any humans, but outsiders like us who do not have immunity from the terrible laws that nature spares its own. That is what we're up against.

I transmit that there are other things I want to do with my days, not take over Tudor Park. Not now, tonight or even tomorrow or whenever he dies from this sickness that makes him want to lie hunched like a fetus. Does he want Tudor Park to be my blessing in life or my curse? Die now and it's a curse, a dreadful burden and a curse. Live, and not die till far off in the future, then that's Tudor Park the blessing. "I want to sing," I pray-whisper. I have a script I will learn. I want to sing on a stage, in my stomach and chest voice that the more I practise becomes strong.

There is anger in my transmission now. Tonight my fate will be decided. If The Duke dies, would I have to leave school? Would I stay in Taonga, marry Bettina? She is probably a gold-digger. She will leave me, and where's his legacy then? What becomes of it if she takes half? "That's what you are condemning me to. All because of my killing a calf and the justice that passed on to us."

If he loves me, he will live. If he loves me, he will face down the justice, face down death. What kind of father would do anything else but *live* in these circumstances!

"I promise this: I will leave Tudor Park if I have to. Walk off and say to hell with carrying it on. Let Norman run it. Let Churchill beat your horses till they're broken and fucking cowed. It will be your fault. It will be because of you."

I make this silent vow to him: if I must become the duke myself I will let my penis go to cock when feeding the calves. I will let them suck and slurp it so when he drifts above me with the other curious ancestors I will have my revenge on him for how terribly I've been wronged.

★

In the emergency ward The Duke resumes his S.

A rugby-sized male nurse wrestles him open to change his clothes from pyjamas to paper smock. A doctor questions him loudly to penetrate the deafness of drugs. "Where exactly is the pain? Point exactly to where there's pain." He politely insists that Feet and I make ourselves comfortable in the waiting room down the corridor, or in the cafeteria to the right and follow the signs. He will visit us when more tests are done. Feet raises her chin as a challenge to bad fortune. Her lip corners turn up a smile of fake confidence. She puts her arm around me as if I might be too frozen to steer my own walking.

In rooms along the corridor humans lie with mouths gaping in snoreless sleep, yellow soles protruding from blankets. Tubes in their noses or the crooks of their arms as if creepers from the walls have got in under them. The paper smocks have a back-split that leaves people's privates glimpseable. Feet refuses to look. She reprimands me that I shouldn't look either. "Hospitals are so depressing," she shivers in her graveyard way. "I can't do anything but pretend I'm not here. The sickness just rubs off on you." She wishes there was a private room we could go to. "I don't mind paying for a little room away from people's staring, people saying with their eyes, 'What's she doing here? She looks a cut above the rest of us, but cut down to size now. She's just like the rest of us now.'"

She unzips her sunglasses from her bag. "I'll be damned if I'll have all these eyes see the state of me."

★

Kidney stones.

"All the worry. All the fuss." Feet slumps in the chair beside The Duke's hospital bed. She removes her sunglasses. She says that we will be laughing stock of Taonga: an ambulance and all that fuss. "I'm even laughing at it myself. Well at least old fancy pants is lucky, they'll have to admit."

The Duke slides up onto pillows. His dentures aren't in. He points Feet to where they are wrapped in tissue. A stalactite of skin hangs like a tip from his pale gum. He sucks the teeth into his mouth like a mouth-guard and boasts that he is not ready yet to push up daisies. He'll push out kidney stones but not push up daisies—we can't get rid of him that easily. He has unfinished business this side of the sod.

Such as winning a Melbourne Cup. And seeing his son married to a woman as beautiful as his own wife. There are those grandchildren he wants to see mucking around in the paddocks. A boy and a girl each, please. A boy to take Tudor Park forward into the years. A girl to help out with the book-keeping. "I've got some big ideas. Buying up our neighbours some day. Expanding our operations through-out the whole of Taonga," he says, sweeping his hand across the air. "Let's make us the biggest agricultural operation in the whole of Australasia. No, bugger it. The biggest oper-ation in the world. A scrape with death just gives me a big-ger appetite for being alive and making a mark that says 'I lived here.'"

He reaches for Feet's hand. He clasps it in his.

"Not so tight," she winces because he has crunched her fingers together painfully against her rings. She leans on his shoulder, careful to settle her hair on the edge of his pillow and not dent her comb-work: "The whole world! I like the sound of that. That's more like the man I married talking."

The Duke reaches for my hand. The bottoms of his eyes are puddling. "And what about you?" he asks me. "What have you got to say for yourself?" Said not as true inquiry but as men speak heartily to men, and a father to his son.

"What have *you* got to say for yourself?" I play along. I want to sing out the relief in me. A me who is not to be duke but freed. I take a breath to let out a deep stomach note for all the hospital to hear, but abort it—if I start singing, Feet will clap her hands together and say, "That's all very nice and good, but what about a bit of Dean Martin? Something special and swoony I can hum."

There is no such thing as prayer transmission or else for what I prayed out to him, the threat of leaving, and cock and calf sin, The Duke would not have his satisfied grin. Nor is there an animal justice—he would not be sitting there if there was. He is hardly a fighter, a warrior to look at, unless you're meant to face down nature with tears welling. Do it with your teeth just put in and talking toughly of owning the world.

"How are those calves of yours?" He squeezes my hand.

"I'm late feeding them today because of you there. I'll have to do it before it gets dark."

The Duke rests his head against Feet's arm and sighs to me, "What a good sense of responsibility you have. I couldn't be happier with the way you're turning out. What a credit you are to yourself, to me and to my lovely lady here."

He urges us to get on our way in a cab so his boy can do his chores, feed his starving calves.

Feet kisses his cheek. He and I shake hands. He compliments my handshake for its controlled power. "Hard work is making a man of you," he says, waving us to get going out into the corridor and back to Tudor Park.

Feet clip-clops along the shiny floor so fast I have to skip into a jogging stride to keep up. She hums as she passes people as if to let them know she is not one of them—poor unfortunates with faces longer than a mile.

She holds out her arm for me to do the right thing and come in under her wing. I let her hold me for a few strides.

"We're back to normal," she says. "That's the main thing. I'm going to have a victory champers the very second that I'm home."

I MIX MILK into the vat on wheels, drive the tractor down the cow race to where the moaning huddlers are paddocked. Miss Beautiful, the loudest of them all as usual. I answer her with singing. I don't care if Norman catches my voice upon the air and performs an off-with-the-fairies eye roll. I let out lungfuls of notes from down in me, so joyfully released that I could bawl in ecstasy. Is this what bliss is? Is this the happiest I have ever been?

I wade through the nuzzling moaners. I knee their mouths from my fly. They seize my fingers and suckle. I have no penis-cock sensation. Is bliss so pure that it washes our imagination clean?

I finger-steer mouths to the vat's boom and tell Miss Beautiful—singing the telling instead of plain talk—that she is as greedy as always; there won't be enough left for others.

But let her be greedy today. Today in my bliss state I can't refuse my darlings their gorging. Today I will mix another batch so they can share my bliss as well. A celebration with milk as their very own champagne toast. I drive back to the milk shed. Re-fill the vat. Return.

The toast for some mouths only lasts a minute before they slide from the rubbers, white saliva suspended to the ground. Others stay a minute more. Miss Beautiful and three larger calves are left to drain the dregs dry.

I stretch out my arms and sing, "Toast that I am free, Miss Beautiful. Free and so you must toast my life," walking towards a ridge where wind pushes me, tries to shove itself inside my body past my voice. The current from inside me is stronger than any wind's power. I win the combat: my voice versus the wind which is reduced to having to grab at my coat and hair. It can't gather enough strength to buffet me backwards.

I walk over the ridge and down the other side as if advancing on the wind to capture it. I stomp dirt-clumps down, leaves, twigs, as if these are the crude weapons of the wind discarded in its hurry. The sun has slipped away at the sight of me. It has ducked behind a tree top slowly as if any sudden movement breaks its cover. But I already saw it and sing so—"There you are, a sun behind a tree." I will leave it to sulk there. I salute it goodbye and sing my way back to the calves.

They are gathered a small distance away from the vat. Gathered in a circle as grown-up cows might ring a water trough and sniff and snort at the surface. They are competing, heads low, to be included in the circle, butting for a place in the crowd. I walk closer. There at the bottom of the circle, a calf on its side, belly globed. A bloated calf. Not any calf. Miss Beautiful.

I slap and screech to be let through into the ring. Miss Beautiful. Her mouth wide open. Milky tongue dangling dead in the grass. Her eyes turned up into bloodshot whites. Legs stuck out like a rubber glove inflated.

I hit her to get a breath back. I twist my fist into her throat to clear a passageway. "Get up. Get up," I hit. "Miss Beautiful. Not you. Not you."

I vomit brine. I chant her name, a howling chant that burns my throat with the strain. I chant that I have killed Miss Beautiful. I punch my head to pass the death down to me. My temples, my jaw, my nose. I punch till blood-snot slimes my lips. I tear my shirt open at the buttons to ram my knuckles into my bare ribs, where the heart is so as to stop it. I fail. I sit. Calves come closer to smell me once I am silent. I am heaving. I have the extra breath again. The scales are even. The Duke survives but the death is passed to Miss Beautiful.

I must drag her with a chain now for the dead cow lorry. "Just a calf. Put it out of your mind," Norman will say. But my mind has no door that goes outwards.

To have one moment with no thought in it. Two moments when I haven't thought a word. A day. A week. A year. No one could fail at something so easy. Not if they had a brain, could they?